MONEY MATTERS IN MARRIAGE

Talking About Money & The Bible

By Peter J. Briscoe

Bible references

Verses are taken from The ESV® Bible (The
Holy Bible, English Standard Version®). ESV® Text Edition:
016.
Copyright © 2001 by Crossway, a publishing ministry of
Good
News Publishers. The ESV® text has been reproduced in
cooperation with and by permission of Good News
Publishers

All other verses are taken from THE HOLY BIBLE,
NEW INTERNATIONAL VERSION®, NIV®
Copyright © 1973, 1978, 1984, 2011 by Biblica, Inc.® Used
by
permission. All rights reserved worldwide.

Money Matters in Marriage

Table of Contents

Introduction

They say that 'money talks.' If that's true, then talking about money in marriage is really needed. This book aims to give you many talking points to start your money conversations. It will help you unlock the currency of conversation and lead you to realise that money matters in marriage!

The book aims to foster open and constructive discussions about finances within marriage, helping couples build stronger connections and shared financial strategies.

It does not try to offer a comprehensive manual on money in marriage but seeks to provide highlights to facilitate talking about important issues, helping couples build stronger connections and shared financial strategies.

Money, in its various forms, holds an undeniable place in the intricacies of our daily lives. From the humblest of households to the richest of estates, it weaves its way into the fabric of existence, impacting our choices, our aspirations, and, indeed, our relationships. Yet, perhaps nowhere is its influence more pronounced and its significance more acute than within the sacred marriage covenant.

The notion that "money matters" takes on a profound meaning within the context of marriage, where financial harmony or discord can either fortify the bonds of love or threaten to unravel them.

In this exploration of "Money Matters in Marriage," we embark on a journey that delves deep into the heart of married life, seeking to understand the role of finances and the impact of financial disagreements. We will also be guided by biblical wisdom principles, which have provided solace, guidance, and a moral compass for countless couples over centuries. These principles, grounded in the enduring teachings of scripture, offer a path towards achieving financial unity, nurturing trust, and fostering an emotionally enriched and financially secure partnership.

Addressing Money Matters in Marriage

Picture a serene and picturesque lake, its waters glistening under the gentle caress of sunlight. On the surface, all seems tranquil, but beneath, powerful currents swirl, shaping the lake's very being. Much like this lake, the exterior of many marriages may appear peaceful, with smiles and tender moments shared, but beneath the surface lies a realm where financial undercurrents can be equally influential.

Money problems often form an emotional battleground in marriage. Money, however, is almost never the real issue. The real issue is about our inner drive and motivation, and a lack of Biblical wisdom about marriage and about money.

Why do we emphasise the importance of addressing these financial matters in marriage? The answer lies in the very nature of matrimony itself. A marriage is a covenant, a union where two individuals become one, sharing dreams, responsibilities, and resources. Financial matters are not external to this covenant but intrinsically woven into its fabric. They concern the heart. Therefore, addressing money matters is not just a practical necessity but an essential component of the commitment between two people who promise to share their lives.

When a man and a woman embark on the path of life, they often come from different financial backgrounds, influenced by their upbringing, experiences, and personal beliefs. The union of these unique financial stories is both an opportunity and a challenge. An opportunity to create a harmonious partnership built on trust and shared aspirations and a challenge to navigate the inevitable differences that arise.

In the following chapters, we will explore how couples can embark on this journey towards financial unity, understanding that it is not the absence of financial challenges defining a successful marriage but how these challenges are met, discussed, and resolved.

The Role of Biblical Principles in Shaping Financial Unity

As we navigate the intricate terrain of "Money Matters in Marriage," we do so with the guidance of timeless wisdom – the wisdom found in the teachings of the Bible. The scriptures, revered by countless individuals and communities, provide a moral compass and ethical framework for living a life that is both righteous and fulfilling. This includes the realm of finances and, by extension, the dynamics of marriage.

Biblical principles offer a blueprint for navigating financial matters within a marital relationship. These principles are rooted in love, trust, honesty, and integrity – values that are foundational to a healthy and harmonious marriage. By grounding our approach to money in these principles, couples can find the path to financial unity.

One of the central themes of biblical teachings regarding money is stewardship. Stewardship is the concept that all we possess, including our finances, is entrusted to us by God. As stewards, we are called to manage our resources wisely, with integrity, and in a way that aligns with what God has revealed to us. This perspective shifts the focus from ownership to responsibility, emphasising the need to use our financial blessings to reflect our values and beliefs.

Another key principle is the recognition that money, in and of itself, is neither inherently good nor evil. It is our choices and intentions that imbue money with moral significance. Scripture teaches us that the love of money, or the pursuit of wealth at the expense of higher values, can lead to moral peril. However, money can also be a powerful tool for good, enabling us to support our families, contribute to charitable causes, and improve the well-being of those in need.

Throughout this exploration of "Money Matters in Marriage," we will draw upon the wisdom of biblical principles to provide guidance on achieving financial unity within a marriage. These principles will serve as our compass, directing us towards a path of trust, shared values, and financial transparency. With these principles as our guide, we embark on a journey to strengthen the bonds of love, deepen the foundation of trust, and ultimately build an emotionally and financially secure partnership.

Writing these chapters has served to remind me to be so thankful for my wife, Didie, and to the Lord - without whom my life would be less meaningful and fulfilling.

Peter J. Briscoe
Leiden, The Netherlands. January 2024

Chapter 1: Money & Marriage - the Foundation

I was standing on the station platform, waiting for the train back home from work- and there she was - wrapped in a long white scarf, long winter coat and white boots. I fell in love.

Long dark hair, dark brown eyes ... beautiful in every way. From that moment—that first moment that I laid eyes on her—I knew my life would never be the same. I knew she was the girl I wanted to marry. Amazingly, she had similar feelings for me! Fifty-one years later, I am more thankful than ever for Didie and the marriage God gave us.

A few years after we married, we joined a Bible study group titled "Two Become One." From that study, we learned much about what the Bible says about marriage. (Later, we translated it into Dutch.)

Our marriage of 51 years has not been all plain sailing! We have known many rough seas and harsh weather. However, God's commitment to us and ours to each other have seen us through some tough times. A particular piece of marriage advice which has meant a lot to me has been, "May your fountain be blessed, and may you rejoice in the wife (*husband*) of your youth." (Proverbs 5:18 -*italics mine*) I have learned to see my wife as a source of strength, encouragement, correction and wisdom. I learned that God didn't give me my wife to frustrate me but to bless and complete me. He has created each of us with needs met by our mate's unique personality. Clearly, Didie and I complement one another; my weaknesses are her strengths, and vice-versa.

Two become One

In God's divine plan for marriage, the equation is simple: one plus one equals one. As Jesus teaches us, "They are no longer two, but one" (Matthew 19:6). This unity extends to every facet of a couple's life – physically, emotionally, spiritually, and financially.

God's design for marriage is a beautiful blend where two individuals become one while retaining their unique personalities and abilities. It's like merging two metals to create a stronger alloy, where independence decreases and interdependence grows. Over a lifetime, couples work to enhance this unity as they share more and more of their lives.

In the sacred covenant of marriage, unity holds paramount significance. It's the coming together of two individuals, not just in body and spirit but in navigating life's journey. This unity encompasses all aspects of existence, including the financial realm. The Bible says, "For this reason, a man will leave his father and mother and be united to his wife, and the two will become one flesh" (Genesis 2:24, NIV). This unity extends to financial matters, and couples must recognise the significance of becoming one in this critical aspect of their lives.

The shared pursuit of a life intertwined with love, respect, and unity necessitates recognising that financial matters are intrinsically woven into its fabric. Therefore, it is not just a practical necessity but an essential component of the commitment between two people who promise to share their lives. By actively addressing financial matters and striving for unity in this realm, couples enhance the strength of their marital bond.

At its core, marriage is a covenant, a sacred agreement, a promise that nothing will break the lifelong commitment made to one another. The exchange of rings symbolises this covenant, and the marriage vow, with phrases like "for richer or poorer, for better or worse, in sickness and in health," affirms unwavering love.

Consider the significance of those last seven words. You are promising, "I will love you no matter what." These words are the sweetest assurance in our imperfect, stumbling, and often sinful human nature. The pledge that someone will stand by us, endure our flaws and quirks, and love us as we learn and grow together is a remarkable gift.

Marital love should be so profound that it mirrors, in some mysterious way, the love Jesus Christ has for His church. As Ephesians 5:31-32 tells us, a man leaves his family to be united with his wife, and they become one flesh, echoing the profound mystery of Christ's love for the church. This "Covenant" encapsulates Christ's love for the church and the essence of marriage.

Regrettably, some enter marriage with an escape hatch mentality, ready to bail if things get tough. We must firmly shut that hatch and commit ourselves wholeheartedly to the marriage God has blessed us with.

Leave and Cleave

Mark and Sarah, deeply in love and married for three years, faced an unyielding challenge in their relationship. Mark's parents held a formidable grip on their lives. His inability to detach from their influence strained their marriage.

Sarah yearned for autonomy, for their home to be their sanctuary, free from external control. But Mark's reluctance to confront his parents about boundaries led to continued interference.

Whether it was financial decisions, career choices, or even where they should spend their vacations, Mark's parents' opinions weighed heavily. This constant presence left Sarah feeling unheard and diminished. Their love for each other was undeniable, but the spectre of his parents' influence loomed large, testing the limits of their commitment. Sarah knew that for their relationship to flourish, Mark had to find the strength to prioritise their partnership over his parents' expectations.

Mark was placing his parents above his wife, which should not happen. Jesus Christ said,

"A man shall leave his father and mother and shall cleave to his wife." (Matthew 19:5). When you marry, you are to leave your parents and cleave to your spouse to become financially and emotionally independent from them. Part of the reason to go is that it forces us to become more mature and dependent on each other and our heavenly Father.

Husband and wife need to cleave to one another. In the original language, the word for "cleave" means to "stick like glue."

When a baby eagle is born, the parents care for it until it is old enough to fly. Then, the mother nudges the young eagle out of the nest, forcing it to use its little wings. Like eagles, parents should encourage their married children to transfer their dependence to the Lord and each other.

The 'one-anothers'

The Bible provides a series of principles that I call the "one-anothers." They reveal how to relate best to each other. Although these principles don't apply exclusively to marriage, they do apply to it.

Try substituting your partner's name for the "one-another" as you consider what would happen if you modelled these!

- "Do nothing from selfishness or empty conceit, but with humility of mind regard one another as more important than yourselves; do not merely look out for your interests, but also for the interests of others." (Philippians 2:3-4)
- "Be at peace with one another." (Mark 9:50)
- "Live in harmony with one another." (Romans 12:16)
- "Let us stop passing judgment on one another." (Romans 14:13)
- "So then let us pursue the things which make for peace, the building up of one another." (Romans 14:19)
- "Accept one another, then, just as Christ accepted you." (Romans 15:7)
- "Serve one another in love." (Galatians 5:13)
- "Carry each other's burdens, and in this way you will fulfil the law of Christ." (Galatians 6:2)
- "Be completely humble and gentle; be patient, bearing with one another in love." (Ephesians 4:2)
- "Be kind and compassionate to one another, forgiving each other, just as Christ God forgave you." (Ephesians 4:32)
- "Do not lie to one another..." (Colossians 3:9)
- "Comfort one another." (1 Thessalonians 4:18)
- "Make sure that nobody pays back wrong for wrong, but always try to be kind to each other." (1 Thessalonians 5:15)
- "Encourage one another . . ." (Hebrews 10:25)

- "Don't grumble against each other...or you will be judged." (James 5:9)
- "Above all, love each other deeply, because love covers a multitude of sins." (1 Peter 4:8)

Love and marriage

"So now faith, hope, and love abide, these three; but the greatest of these is love." (1 Corinthians 13:13)

Money is like love. It slowly and painfully destroys the one who withholds it and enriches the one who uses it for the good of their neighbour. To love is to give. If you choose money over love, you will always be poor. We need to love people and use money instead of loving money and using people!

Someone quipped, "You can use money to buy a dog, but only love will make it wag its tail!"

The Greek word for love is 'agape,' which means sacrificial giving - generosity that costs. We offer, not out of duty or compulsion but because we love God. Giving is the logical reaction to the fact that God loved us first and gave us the most precious gift—salvation through the sacrifice of Jesus.

'*Agape*' love is not an emotion but more a devotion. Not a feeling but a conscious choice. C.S. Lewis wrote, "Being in love is a good thing, but it is not the best thing... Love...is a deep unity maintained by the will and deliberately strengthened by habits reinforced by the grace which both partners ask and receive from God. On this love, the engine of marriage is run; being in love was the explosion that started it."[1]

Biblical love is a commitment to sacrifice for each other willingly.

God elevates the importance of love in 1 Corinthians 13:4-7. "Love is patient, love is kind. It does not envy, it does not boast, it is not proud. It does not dishonour others; it is not self-seeking; it is not easily angered; it keeps no record of wrongs. Love does not delight in evil but rejoices with the truth. It always protects, always trusts, always hopes, always perseveres."

What could this passage mean for money in marriage? Here is a suggestion of how to commit based on this description of love in action in money matters.

1. **Love is Patient:** "We will be patient with each other, giving each other the time and space needed to grow and overcome challenges together. We will avoid impulsive financial decisions but wait on one another and the Lord for His guidance."

2. **Love is Kind:** "We commit to showing kindness in our words and actions, supporting and uplifting each other through life's ups and downs. We will be generous and help those in need."

3. **It Does Not Envy:** "We will celebrate each other's successes and joys rather than being envious or competitive in our relationship. We will not envy what others have but focus on our God-given goals."

4. **It Does Not Boast:** "We will not boast about our wealth or financial successes, but be modest and respectful of others' financial situations."

5. **It Is Not Proud:** "We promise to remain humble, always valuing and respecting each other as equals in our marriage, listening to one another's ideas and valuing their experience. We will seek financial advice and make well-informed decisions."

6. **It Does Not Dishonor Others:** "We will respect each other's feelings, boundaries, and dignity, avoiding actions that

dishonour our relationship. We will treat each other respectfully, whether discussing spending or negotiating financial matters.

7. **It Is Not Self-Seeking:** "We commit to considering each other's needs and desires rather than focusing solely on our individual interests. We will listen to others' advice and be open to different financial strategies rather than insisting on our own financial path."

8. **It Is Not Easily Angered**: "We will strive to remain patient and understanding, avoiding unnecessary anger and hostility in our interactions. We will avoid reacting emotionally to financial setbacks and strive to maintain emotional stability in making sound financial decisions.

9. **It Keeps No Record of Wrongs**: "We pledge not to hold onto grudges, but to forgive and move forward, offering each other a clean slate." We will seek to understand and forgive."

10. **Love Does Not Delight in Evil**: "We will not engage in or condone actions that harm our relationship but will uphold a standard of love and goodness in all we do. We will avoid unethical financial practices. And focus on financial integrity."

11. **It Rejoices with the Truth:** "We will celebrate honesty and transparency in our marriage, always seeking the truth and embracing it."

12. **It Always Protects**: "We commit to protecting each other emotionally, physically, and spiritually, ensuring that our marriage remains a safe haven."

13. **Always Trusts**: "We promise to trust in each other's intentions, keeping faith in our love and relying on each other's support."

14. **Always Hopes**: "We will maintain hope in our shared future, supporting each other's dreams and aspirations. We will set financial goals under the Lord's guidance and work towards them with faith and trust."

15. **Always Perseveres:** "We commit to persevering through life's challenges together, never giving up on our love

and the bond we share. When faced with financial setbacks, we will persevere. We will not give up on our financial aspirations but continue to work towards a stable and prosperous financial future."

These commitments can serve as a strong foundation for a loving and enduring marriage built on the principles of 1 Corinthians 13.

Chapter 2. How God uses money

Here's the big picture: God intends married couples to use money—even challenges with money, even crises with money—to bring them closer rather than separating them. Unfortunately, many couples experience money as a wedge that divides them, but God intends money to be the glue that bonds your love for each other.

God loves and cares deeply for you. And that's why the Bible has so much to say about money. It contains 2,350 verses dealing with money and possessions, and 15 per cent of everything that Jesus Christ said had to do with it. God knows that money will be a struggle for all of us from time to time, and He wants to equip us to handle it well. And the Bible is equally practical regarding how to have a great marriage. God designed marriage to be a blessing.

God uses money in three ways - as a tool, a test and a testimony.

- As a tool to assess our capacity to use money well.

In Matthew 25, God gives large amounts of money to three stewards expected to do business with what they have been entrusted with. To those who used the money well, according to the master's wishes, the master complimented them. The reward of good stewardship was more stewardship! "Well done, good and faithful servant. You have been faithful over a little; I will set you over much." (Matthew 25:23) The reward was also 'the joy of the master.'

    - As a test to assess our faithfulness in using the money in the right way, especially with the little we are entrusted with. "One who is faithful in a very little is also faithful in much, and one who is dishonest in a very little is also dishonest in much." (Luke 16:10) . The extent to which we will be trusted with what Jesus called "the true riches" is to a large extent determined by how well we use the money entrusted to us. "If then you have not been faithful in the unrighteous wealth, who will entrust to you the true riches?" (Luke 16:11) And the extent to which we will be given more money to manage is also determined by how faithful we are in managing Gods money as a trusted steward. "And if you have not been faithful in that which is another's, who will give you that which is your own?" (Luke 16: 12)

    - As a testimony to each other and those around us as they see God working through our lives as we trust Him in our financial decisions. It is an excellent testimony to our Lord when we live a life of contentment and thankfulness despite difficult circumstances and when we are generous and share what we have to alleviate the needs of others.

An outside indicator

God uses money to get an indication of our heart's priorities. My good friend, Dr. Andres Panasiuk, said, "What we do with our money is an outward indicator of an inward spiritual condition." The basis of this statement can be found in Jesus' words, "For where your treasure is, there your heart will be also."

(Matthew 6:21) Jesus is saying that the way you spend money is a direct reflection of what you consider to be most important. Your money follows your heart and vice-versa. As the Lord is primarily concerned with our hearts, he is keen to see how we manage our money!

Someone once challenged me. "Show me your bank statements, and I will show you what you live for!" Bank statements show, in black and white, our priorities because we direct our money to that which brings us what we desire and need most. He said, "If you say that God is number one in your life, and this is not reflected in your bank statements, then you are fooling yourself!"
Your money follows your heart!

Navigating our finances is a partnership between me, my spouse and the Lord! Each has a unique part to play.

The Husband's Unique Role

The most crucial role of the husband is to love his wife. This love is to be characterised by serving and caring. The Bible expresses it this way: "Husbands, love your wives, just as Christ loved the church and gave himself up for her . . . husbands ought to love their wives as their own bodies. He who loves his own wife loves himself" (Ephesians 5:25, 28). It is a sacrificial love.

I remember the founder of Compass, Howard Dayton, telling about his wife's struggle with cancer and how he helped nurse her through this immensely challenging time. Howard had a very fruitful ministry, travelling worldwide and teaching people about Biblical finances. Someone asked him, "Aren't you disappointed you cannot travel as much and continue leading Compass? "No. He replied. "This is a wonderful opportunity to serve Bev, my wife. This is now my priority."

He encouraged us, "View every request by your wife as an opportunity to serve her! When Bev asks me to do something for her, if possible, I stop what I'm doing and immediately do it. And I've discovered something surprising. I experience joy when serving her. The Lord made us, as husbands, to sacrificially serve our wives, and when we do, we sense His pleasure."

I've remembered those words and do my best to put this example into practice.

When God calls people to unite, He designates a leader for the journey. In the sacred bond of marriage, God has chosen the husband as the head of the wife. As stated in Ephesians 5:23, "The husband is the head of the wife as Christ is the head of the church." It's vital to emphasise that the husband's role doesn't imply superiority; rather, it signifies different God-given functions, each equally valuable.

This aspect can be delicate for couples, particularly when a husband has yet to wholeheartedly demonstrate sacrificial love and service to his wife. In such cases, she might feel unappreciated and insecure. When a husband's leadership tilts towards control rather than compassion, it can trigger resistance from his wife.

A husband's leadership approach should not be overbearing or authoritarian. Instead, it should be marked by understanding and bestowing honour upon his wife. As articulated in 1 Peter 3:7, "Husbands... be considerate as you live with your wives, and treat them with respect as the weaker partner and as heirs with you of the gracious gift of life, so that nothing will hinder your prayers."

I had the privilege of speaking with Dr. Frits Phillips, grandson of the founder of the famous electronics concern and, at that time, CEO of the corporation. He said, "Whoever does not ask their wife for advice misses half of God's blessings!" He based this on the verse just quoted. They are 'heirs with you of the gracious gift of life,' meaning that God bestows His gifts and grace on both marriage partners equally.

In fulfilling his role as the head, the husband must obediently serve God and prioritise his wife above other commitments, including children, friends, recreation, ministry, or career. Emotional absence or passivity is not an option. Instead, he should actively seek to protect her, even in challenging situations, such as shielding her from harassing phone calls by unsympathetic creditors.

Around my 30th, I was CEO of a chemical company, travelling a lot over Europe. Due to the pressures of work and the travel burden, I was neglecting my wife at home, who had three small children to care for. At that time, I took time to evaluate what I was doing and concluded: "A success in business, but a failure at life." After that, I changed my focus to put family needs ahead of business. I have spoken with many people at the end of their careers, and no one ever commented, "I wish I'd have spent more time in the office." It is almost always, "I wish I'd have spent more time with my family."

The Wife's Unique Role

By God's design, the wife is to help her husband. She should assist, encourage, and respect him. "The Lord God said, 'It is not good for the man to be alone; I will make a helper [woman] suitable for him'" (Genesis 2:18).

The classic example of a wife helping her husband is described in Proverbs 31:10-26.

- "An excellent wife...does [her husband] good and not evil all the days of her life...
- She brings her food from afar.
- She rises also while it is still night and gives food to her household.
- She considers a field and buys it; from her earnings, she plants a vineyard.
- She extends her hand to the poor.
- She makes linen garments, sells them, and supplies belts to the tradesmen."

Think about this wife's extraordinary accomplishments. She provided food and clothing to her family. She was an entrepreneur with a thriving clothing business. She was a successful investor in real estate.

What motivates this industrious wife? Proverbs 31:27 reveals, "She looks well to the ways of her household." She wants to help her husband by managing the home and earning extra money. I love how he and the children honour her: "Her children arise and call her blessed; her husband also, and he praises her: Many women do noble things, but you surpass them all." (Proverbs 31:28,-29)

Her husband's leadership style allowed for the full expression of his wife's talents. Husbands, how would you describe your leadership style? Does it encourage your wife to be all she can be within her role as your helper, or are you stifling her God-given talents and creativity?

Wives, are you fulfilling your role of helping your husband?

Another aspect of a wife's role is to embrace her husband's leadership. Ephesians 5:22 and 24 suggest, "Wives, submit to your husbands as to the Lord... as the church submits to Christ, so also wives should submit to their husbands in everything."

Some think that submission means never expressing an opinion or doing just what the husband demands, but that's not what is intended. It means respecting your husband enough to follow his leadership.

It may be challenging to grasp, but God's desire is for wives to respect and submit, even if their husbands have not embraced Jesus Christ as their Saviour or perhaps know Him but struggle to obey Him.

"Wives . . . be submissive to your husbands so that, if any of them do not believe the word, they may be won over without words by the behaviour of their wives . . . Your beauty . . . should be that of . . . a gentle and quiet spirit, which is of great worth in God's sight. For this is the way the holy women of the past who put their hope in God used to make themselves beautiful. They were submissive to their own husbands, like Sarah, who obeyed Abraham and called him her master. You are her daughters if you do what is right and do not give way to fear." (1 Peter 3:1-7)

The closing words of the passage hold a vital message: "You are her daughters if you do what is right and do not give way to fear." It can indeed be daunting when your husband's financial choices deviate from God's principles. However, trust God's love and provision instead of succumbing to fear. When you align with your husband's leadership and trust in the Lord, His transformative work can bring about positive change in your husband's life and financial circumstances, ultimately leading to good.

God's role in your marriage

The Bible reveals a clear division of responsibilities in the handling of money. Simply put, God has specific responsibilities and has given others to us. Much of the frustration we experience in our finances comes from not realising which responsibilities are ours and which are not.

The Lord's primary responsibility is that He owns all your stuff! He created and owns everything. Psalm 24:1 says, "The earth is the Lord's, and everything in it."

Richard and Wendy Gray, a couple living in a cosy suburban neighbourhood, experienced a pivotal moment that would forever change how they viewed their money and possessions. It all began with studying the Compass course, "Navigating Finances - God's Way," which astonished them.

One evening, a sense of curiosity overcame them as they sat in their living room. Wendy turned to Richard with a perplexed expression. "You mean that Richard and I don't own anything?" she inquired. Her voice held a mixture of wonder and disbelief.

Richard, equally baffled, gazed at his wife. "The home, the car, the savings—none of it's ours; it's all God's?" he echoed her questions, searching for clarity. "We've always thought as long as we give 10 per cent of our income, we can spend 90 per cent any way we want."

They both realised that their perspective on ownership had been drastically altered. If God was indeed the Owner of everything, it meant a profound shift in their approach to possessions. Their understanding led them to the conviction that they needed to manage all they had in a manner that would please God. It was a revelation that gave them a sense of responsibility and a newfound dedication to align their financial decisions with their faith.

Understanding God's ownership of all we possess can be a concept we accept intellectually yet struggle to fully embrace in our daily lives. It's a paradox we face.

Consider this: the world around us, including our neighbours, the media, and even the legal system, constantly reinforces the idea that we own our possessions. It's a prevailing narrative. However, when we turn to the Bible, we encounter a profound revelation—the ultimate truth that God is the rightful Owner of all we have!

God, Our Provider

The Lord's promise to provide for our needs remains unwavering. As stated in Matthew 6:33 (NIV), "Seek first His kingdom and His righteousness, and all these things [food and clothing] shall be given to you."

This is the same God who graciously provided manna to sustain the children of Israel throughout their 40 years of wandering in the wilderness. The same God miraculously fed 5,000 people with only five loaves and two fish. His history of provision is rich and enduring.

Recall the story of Elijah, to whom the Lord declared, "I have commanded the ravens to provide for you... The ravens brought him bread and meat in the morning and bread and meat in the evening" (1 Kings 17:4, 6).

God's faithfulness in meeting our needs is predictable, but His methods often surprise us. His provision may come in various forms, such as an increase in income, unexpected gifts, or opportunities to make the most of limited resources through wise and thrifty purchases. While we cannot foresee the precise means, we can always rely on His steadfast care and provision.

This three-way partnership in managing money is strong!

"Two are better than one, because they have a good reward for their toil. For if they fall, one will lift up his fellow. But woe to him who is alone when he falls and has not another to lift him up! Again, if two lie together, they keep warm, but how can one keep warm alone? And though a man might prevail against one who is alone, two will withstand him—a threefold cord is not quickly broken." (Ecclesiastes 4:9-12)

Chapter 3. Getting to know you

Opposites attract. More often than not, each partner brings very different aspects of their personality, history and values to their marriage. Each partner is unique, and marriage brings together two people with differing outlooks on life, other perspectives on money and often unspoken expectations from their partner.

Claire and Daniel each had different money personalities. Claire was meticulous and frugal. She had a detailed budget for every aspect of her life and never spent a penny without careful consideration. Her savings account was her pride and joy, and she meticulously tracked every expense to ensure she never went over budget.

Daniel, on the other hand, was spontaneous and carefree. Money was meant to be enjoyed, and he tended to live for the moment. He had a knack for finding unique experiences and often surprised himself with impulsive purchases.

They met at a friend's party. The contrast in their money personalities was immediately evident as Claire thoughtfully sipped her drink and Daniel animatedly shared tales of his recent travel adventures. They talked, and though their perspectives on finances clashed, there was a spark.

In the early days of their marriage, their differences caused some friction. Claire felt overwhelmed by Daniel's spending habits, while he found her budgeting approach stifling. They had their share of disagreements about money.

But as time passed, they began to appreciate each other's qualities. Claire realised that Daniel brought excitement and spontaneity into her life, while Daniel found that Claire's financial discipline had its merits. They decided to find a way to balance their money personalities.

They established a system: a shared account for joint expenses and separate accounts for personal spending. Claire stuck to her budget for essentials, while Daniel had some freedom to spend as he wanted.

As the years passed, they began to complement each other beautifully. Claire's careful planning allowed them to save for their future, while Daniel's sense of adventure brought extra joy into their lives. They found a happy medium where they both felt financially secure and fulfilled.

It wasn't always easy, but their love and willingness to adapt allowed them to find harmony in their financial journey. Claire and Daniel discovered that love could bridge the gap between their different money personalities, creating a life rich in experiences and stability.

Different perspectives can bring conflict, and it is well known that money is one of the most common sources of disagreements and arguments in marriage. God has not purposed us to compete but to complete one another.

God made us unique, with different characters, yet He wants us to become one and live our married lives in unity. Therefore, it is vital to understand each other and to know what has affected our way of handling money. We need to learn to understand what makes the other half 'tick,' what motivates them, how they react in certain circumstances and why they do what they do.

Our attitudes and emotions towards money have mainly been determined by our experiences in early life. These form our 'money story.' Knowing each other's money story is very helpful in understanding what we are bringing to the table and how we have been wired to handle money.

In the words of the old song by Bobby Vinton, "To know, know, know you, is to love, love, love you…"

Your Money Story

Your "Money Story" describes your relationship with money. It tells of the pain, the joy, and the learning and is as unique as you are. It tells of the emotional wounds and highs. It describes how events and people of the past have influenced your view of money.

When I was 15, my father lost his job, I was never told the circumstances, but we had to move from one day to the next to go and live with my aunt. I could only take what I could carry, meaning I had to leave all my possessions behind. Later, they were sold. This has had a long-lasting effect on me. Almost 60 years later, I still hold possessions very lightly, realising that they are only temporary. It is very easy for me to give stuff away. (Sometimes even my wife's stuff also!) My parents had debts they could not pay and went bankrupt I also vowed never to borrow for consumer items. The only borrowing I ever undertook was a mortgage for a home. Through hard work and endurance, my parents were able to put me through university without any loans. These experiences as a kid stayed with me. To my knowledge, our children have likewise never entered into consumer debt.

With money, as with so many other things in life, our hearts are not a clean slate, not a blank piece of paper. There is a lot of stuff already written there, good, bad and sometimes ugly. Each of us has a hotchpotch of money experiences that begin in childhood and continue into adolescence and adulthood.

Our early money experiences influence our adult attitudes and actions around money, and in turn, they will affect others with whom we interact financially. When we begin to piece our money memories and experiences together and explore what they mean to us, we are beginning to learn our money stories.

Money stories are the beliefs we developed early in our lives about money and prosperity. We learn these mostly from our families. These early beliefs create our reality – including what we believe is possible. Our subconscious mind adopts these long-held beliefs, and this becomes the money story we believe to be true.

Your Money Story includes your strengths and challenges with money, arising from your unique circumstances, wiring, and personality type. It consists of all of the sensations, emotions and physical reactions that money stirs within you.

You want to understand your feelings about money because your past experiences, emotions/feelings, thoughts and beliefs will drive your behaviour – consciously and unconsciously.

It is important to understand that this is not emotional archaeology! We are not digging up the past for its own sake. We learn to tell our money stories by putting together the pieces from the past to better understand our relationship with money in the present. We always ask, "How does this memory and the feelings I associate with it still shape my attitudes toward money today?"

Share Your Money Story

Many people aren't fully aware of their money stories' good and bad parts. They experience happiness or frustration at the results. So, how do you find out what your money story is? This is more an 'innercise' than an 'exercise.'

Looking back at your experiences growing up, ask yourselves these questions:

1. What are one or two of your earliest memories of money as a child? Did your family have money or never enough?

2. What role models did you have? What was your parents' relationship with money?

3. Was money talked about in your home, or was it taboo? Was money a cause of anxiety for you as a child? Does one particular memory stand out for you?

4. Did you have pocket money? If so, did you earn it, or was it given to you?

5. Did you work before leaving school? A Saturday job? A paper round? What did you like to spend your money on?

6. What was your first job when you left school? How much did you earn? Do you remember what you spent the first week's wages on?

7. In a relationship with a friend or a sibling, did you and your friend/sibling have similar or different attitudes to money? What were the causes of tension and disagreement, and how did you resolve them?

8. What have you heard about money (a sermon, small group or a particular project) in church? Has the church been influential in shaping your money story?

9.   Think of one large item you bought. What was it, and how did buying it make you feel?

10.   Have you ever regretted buying something? What made you do it?

Share your answers to these questions.

What's your money temperament?

A temperament is your basic nature, which permanently affects your behaviour. Acknowledging each other's temperaments and how they can lead to conflict or collaboration and influence financial habits is paramount in fostering marital harmony.

To achieve harmony, both partners should come to a shared understanding of fundamental principles:

• We recognise that God has designed us with distinct temperaments.

• We acknowledge the unique roles that God has assigned to each of us.

• We understand that our purpose is to complement one another, not compete.

Below is a concise overview of each personality profile, accompanied by critical characteristics that influence financial behaviour. This section is ideal for mutual exploration.

At the end of each profile description, you'll also find examples from the Bible that illustrate these temperament types.

Dominant - Choleric Money Management

Cholerics are clear about their life goals and unhesitatingly express their displeasure when expectations aren't met. When they set financial objectives, they pursue them relentlessly, much like a heat-seeking missile, leaving no stone unturned until the task is accomplished. They are often the most visionary and will stop at nothing to reach their goals.

While their unwavering determination is an asset, cholerics may sometimes need to pay more attention to their spouse in the process, as their focus on the task can lead to a lack of consultation with others. This can occasionally create tension when the partner feels excluded or unheard, only learning of decisions made after the fact.

To achieve a financial goal, cholerics may become workaholics, unable to rest until the mission is accomplished. They excel in negotiation, securing better deals, and efficiently attaining their objectives. Their "never give up" attitude can propel them up the career ladder.

Women in the Bible	Men in the Bible
Sarah, Abraham's wife,	Paul, John the Baptist
Rahab, Rachel, Lydia,	Joshua, Stephen,

Influential - Sanguine Money Management

Sanguines, with their extroverted nature, often excel as natural salespeople. They thrive on building relationships and expanding their social circles. They may adopt an "easy come, easy go" mentality regarding finances.

Among the four personality types, sanguines are most likely to come home with a new car one day just because their neighbour bought a similar one. While it might have been a good deal, their more practical spouse may have preferred to wait, allowing their current car to depreciate further.

Beyond impulse purchases for themselves, sanguines tend to be exceptionally generous. They often prioritise others over themselves, a virtue that may sometimes frustrate their partner who manages the household finances.

Sanguines face their most significant financial challenge in maintaining a balanced budget and consistently setting aside savings and retirement funds. They may benefit from a monthly allowance to help them adhere to a budget and achieve their financial goals.

Women in the Bible	Men in the Bible
Mary Magdalene	Aaron, King Saul, David
Rebekah, Abigail	Peter, Barnabas

Steady - Melancholic Money Management

Melancholics often embody the traits of a perfectionist. They are inclined to create meticulous budgets, which may become so rigid in their quest for flawlessness that they need help to adhere to them. When they do encounter difficulties, it can lead to temporary frustration.

Their pursuit of perfection sometimes causes them to miss out on life experiences due to the fear of failure. Financially, melancholics tend to be frugal, yet they are willing to make substantial purchases in categories they hold in high regard. For instance, they might opt for "the best" when purchasing a new car, invest in designer jeans for clothing, and choose Starbucks over a more affordable café for their coffee fix.

Overall, melancholic spenders are adept at stretching their dollars but won't hesitate to splurge on things they highly value. For couples with a melancholic partner, one of the significant challenges lies in taking risks and venturing beyond their professional and financial comfort zones.

Women in the Bible	Men in the Bible
Dorcas, Martha,	Isaac, Jacob,
Anna, Hannah	Nehemiah, Abraham

Cautious - Phlegmatic money management

The phlegmatic temperament can be considered "Melancholy Lite," exhibiting similar traits but different approaches to risk and spending.

Phlegmatic partners are natural savers and generally live well within their means. While this penchant for saving may be perceived as stinginess, it's important to note that they can be generous when they see the value in a purchase or donation.

One challenge for phlegmatic spouses is avoiding the label of being excessively frugal. While they don't set out to mimic Ebenezer Scrooge, they might benefit from learning to choose gifts that exceed the 99-cent mark for their spouse.

Phlegmatics can also gain a reputation as "packrats" because they tend to hold onto items until they break down. They may acquire second-hand items like couches, clothing, or electronics that others no longer want but are still functional, often to postpone the purchase of something new. One person's trash becomes a phlegmatic's treasure.

With a perfectionist streak, phlegmatics may undertake tasks like investing or saving for a goal. Still, they might require motivation from their choleric or sanguine partner to develop a consistent monthly contribution habit. Once initiated, phlegmatics are known for their unwavering dedication and loyalty.

Women in the Bible	Men in the Bible
Esther, Mary	Luke, John, Thomas,
Ruth	Elijah, Moses

Knowing each other's personality profile will ease tension in the relationship and lower expectations. You will be successful in complimenting each other rather than competing in managing money.

Do this online test separately, and then discuss the results with your partner.

http://www.temperaments.fighunter.com/?page=test

Merging Money Personalities

Marriage is a union of hearts, minds, and, yes, wallets. Financial compatibility is crucial to creating a harmonious life in every relationship. But what happens when you and your partner have different money personalities? How do you merge your unique approaches to money while staying true to your faith? In this article, we'll explore how to combine your money personalities to manage your finances from a biblical perspective.

Steve and Susan, a young couple deeply in love, decided to merge their finances. They found themselves sitting at their cosy kitchen table, a stack of bills and a notepad in front of them. The atmosphere was a blend of excitement and apprehension.

As they began sifting through their financial matters, they realised they had distinctly different money personalities. Meticulous and cautious, Steve had always been a saver who found comfort in a well-structured budget. On the other hand, Susan was a free spirit, finding joy in spontaneity and the pleasures of life.

In their heart-to-heart conversation, they discussed their approaches to money, financial goals, and fears. Susan explained how budget constraints had sometimes stifled her sense of adventure while Steve shared his concerns about future financial security.

Their dialogue was a mix of understanding and compromise. Steve agreed to be more open to the occasional spontaneous splurge, and Susan was willing to work with a more structured budget for their shared financial goals.

As they wrapped up their conversation, they realised their differing money personalities didn't need to drive them apart. Instead, they could be the complementary pieces that complete their financial puzzle, enriching their life with a balance of security and adventure.

When partners do not understand each other's financial types.

Conflict and Resentment: Misunderstanding or ignorance of each other's financial types can lead to frequent conflicts and growing resentment. One partner may perceive the other as careless or overly frugal, causing tension and disagreements.

1. **Financial Stress:** Lack of understanding can result in financial stress. One partner's spending habits may cause financial strain, leaving the other feeling anxious and burdened by the consequences of overspending or excessive saving.

2. **Lack of Trust:** Trust is crucial in any relationship, and trust can be eroded when financial types are not understood. Suspicion may arise if one partner feels the other is hiding expenses or making financial decisions without transparency.

3. **Impact on Future Goals:** Different financial types can lead to conflicting priorities regarding long-term goals. One partner may prioritise saving for a house, while the other may prefer to spend on travel or leisure. This misalignment can hinder the achievement of shared goals.

4. **Communication Breakdown:** Inadequate understanding of each other's financial types can lead to communication breakdown. Partners may avoid discussing financial matters to prevent conflicts, ultimately hindering open and healthy communication within the relationship.

Partners must recognise and respect each other's financial types and work together to find a balanced approach that accommodates both perspectives. Open and honest communication, compromise, and financial planning can address these problems and build a more harmonious relationship.

Biblical Wisdom for Financial Harmony

·   Communication (Proverbs 15:22): The Bible emphasises the importance of seeking counsel, which also applies to financial matters. Open and honest communication is critical to resolving differences in money personalities. Regularly discuss your financial goals, concerns, and priorities.

·   Unity (Genesis 2:24): "That is why a man leaves his father and mother and is united to his wife, and they become one flesh." This verse highlights the unity in marriage. When it comes to finances, it means aligning your financial goals and approaches to money.

·   Understanding (1 Peter 3:7): "Husbands, in the same way be considerate as you live with your wives." This principle applies to both spouses. It's crucial to understand and respect your partner's money personality. Rather than trying to change them, appreciate their unique approach.

Steps to Combine Money Personalities

·   **Prayer and Reflection**: Begin your journey by seeking God's guidance through prayer and reflection. Ask for wisdom and understanding in managing your finances as a couple.

·   **Set Common Goals:** Define your financial goals and priorities as a team. What do you both want to achieve? Whether saving for a home, investing for the future, or giving to charity, create a shared vision.

·   **Budget Together**: Work on a budget incorporating both partners' money personalities. This may involve setting aside funds for spending, saving, and investing, allowing each personality to express itself within a structured framework.

- **Compromise**: Understand that finding financial harmony might require compromise. For example, the spender may agree to a more structured budget, while the saver might be more flexible in certain areas.
- **Financial Accountabilit**y: Hold each other accountable for adhering to your financial plan. Regularly review your budget, track expenses, and make adjustments as needed.
- **Education and Growth**: Encourage each other to learn about finances and grow in financial wisdom. Attend financial seminars or workshops together and share what you've learned.

Combining your money personalities is a beautiful opportunity for growth and unity in marriage. You can navigate your unique money personalities and achieve financial harmony by aligning your approach to finances with biblical principles of communication, unity, stewardship, and understanding. Remember, it's not about changing each other but about honouring your individuality while working together towards shared financial goals.

Looking at money differently

As we have seen, it's important to recognise that you and your spouse probably look at money differently.

We all have strengths, and we all have weaknesses. These differences can be caused by our gender, background, personality and relationship with God. The failure of couples to understand how these differences impact their financial attitudes can lead to deep hurt. However, when husband and wife recognise these differences, they can rely upon the other's strengths to compensate for their weaknesses.

Gender Differences

Husbands and wives are hardwired differently, and that's a good thing. As the late Larry Burkett used to say in jest, "If the husband and wife were both the same, one of them would be unnecessary!"

Gender differences significantly influence how individuals approach and manage money. Society has long assigned gender-based roles and expectations, which can impact financial habits.

Men often exhibit a greater inclination for risk-taking, which can manifest in investment choices. They may be more prone to invest in stocks or other high-risk assets. Conversely, women are generally more risk-averse, often opting for safer, low-yield investments or keeping more of their wealth in cash or bonds.

Communication about money also varies. Men may be more direct in discussing finances, while women tend to be more open to seeking advice and collaboration.

Furthermore, income disparities between genders persist, impacting how each manages their money. Women, on average, earn less than men, which can lead to different spending and saving patterns.

Overcoming gender biases and working toward financial equality is essential. Recognising and valuing diverse financial approaches can lead to more balanced and harmonious money management within relationships and society as a whole.

The second difference between men and women is that most husbands feel the burden of providing for the family. They take 1 Timothy 5:8 to heart, "If anyone does not provide for his relatives, and especially for his immediate family, he has denied the faith and is worse than an unbeliever." Providing is one of the primary ways they express their love to their wives and children.

My Dad, Harold, lost his job. He had been a hardworking and devoted husband and had always taken pride in providing a good life for his family. He had a good job as an accountant that enabled our family to live well in a nice home and could afford for my brother and me to attend good schools. It was a role he cherished.

However, life took an unexpected turn when he lost his job. Suddenly, the financial burden shifted. My mother, Amy, had to take on extra hours to make ends meet, and the family had to severely cut back on our expenses.

The weight of being unable to provide as he once did began to take its toll on my Dad. He felt a profound sense of inadequacy as he felt he was failing his family. Sleepless nights and silent worries became his companions.

Seeing her husband's struggle, my Mum offered unwavering support and reassurance. She showed that their love and unity were more valuable than any financial setback. With her encouragement, my Dad eventually found a new job with lesser pay, but the experience taught them the importance of resilience and showed them the strength of their marriage.

This challenging period in their lives had brought them even closer. Dad realised that being a provider wasn't solely about finances; it was about being there for his family, no matter the circumstances.

Background differences

Differences in upbringing can significantly influence a couple's dynamics. Each partner brings unique family values, communication styles, and expectations into the relationship. Varied experiences can lead to misunderstandings or conflict but also offer growth opportunities. Understanding and respecting these differences is essential. For instance, one partner may come from a family that openly expresses emotions, while the other may come from a more reserved background. These disparities can affect how they communicate and handle conflicts. However, through open dialogue and empathy, couples can learn from each other's backgrounds, enriching their relationship with diverse perspectives and building a stronger, more inclusive partnership.

My wife and I could not have grown up in families that differed more. Didie was raised in a small apartment, sharing a bedroom with the washing machine! She made her own clothes and tirelessly helped her mother keep the house and care for her four brothers. She had to be very careful to stretch every cent.

My parents were quite well off. We could live in lovely homes, buy what we wanted, and spend enjoyable holidays as a family.

Didie taught me to spend less and to think twice before buying something. She learned to spend more. I remember telling my daughters not to come back shopping with their mother unless she had bought something for herself.

Discuss your backgrounds with each other and evaluate how your parents' financial attitudes have influenced you. What influences have been healthy, and which ones have not? How can you work together to utilise the positive influences?

Spiritual differences
Addressing spiritual disparities is essential for a couple to achieve true financial unity. Often, there's a significant variance in financial perspectives between a believer in Jesus Christ and a non-believer. Even among Christians, differences can be substantial, particularly when one is devoted to following Christ while the other is less committed. The most profound dimensions of marital intimacy at the spiritual level are only fully realised through the transformative power of Jesus Christ.

Chapter 4. Money talks, so should we!

Newlyweds, Amelia and Robert grappled with an issue causing tension in their marriage. As they sat down one evening, sharing their thoughts, it became apparent that their differing upbringing significantly impacted their financial discussions.

Amelia's parents had been discreet about money matters during childhood, avoiding financial conversations altogether. In contrast, Robert had grown up in a household where money was a constant source of contention. His parents frequently argued about finances, leaving a lasting imprint on Robert's memory.

Robert confessed, "Amelia and I struggle to discuss money. It's like we're stuck in patterns from our childhood. Tensions run high. She often gets upset, and I tend to withdraw. We've got a lot of emotional baggage regarding money, and it's challenging to have open conversations about our true feelings."

Amelia nodded in agreement, acknowledging the difficulty they faced. "We have to find a way to move past this if we want to make any progress and maintain peace in our marriage."

They were acutely aware that their contrasting financial upbringing had laid the groundwork for discord in their relationship. However, they were determined to liberate themselves from these entrenched patterns and pave the way for a more wholesome and harmonious financial future. Armed with open and honest communication and a mutual dedication to surmount their pasts, they embarked on a shared journey.

Good, intentional communication is essential to maintain unity in marriage. Jesus said, "Every kingdom divided against itself is laid waste, and no city or house divided against itself will stand." (Matthew 12:25) The key to not being divided is to communicate well with each other.

In relationships, speaking honestly and openly is of utmost importance. Many individuals, even within the confines of marriage, shy away from revealing their genuine emotions. They might utter phrases like, "I find budgets to be a hassle," when their real concern is, "I fear that a budget will curtail my spending desires."
Being transparent about your feelings allows you to recognise and address disparities, facilitating constructive dialogue. This approach nurtures an environment that fosters a healthier and more resilient marriage.

Money Dates for Couples

A 'money date' can genuinely transform your relationship and financial well-being and be a game-changer for your relationship.

Peter, a chemist, and Anne, a local politician, believed every aspect of their life should reflect their faith. It was no different when it came to their finances. They had seen how financial discord could tear couples apart and were determined not to let that happen to them.

So, one day, they made a pact. They decided to have regular "money dates," where they would discuss their finances openly, just as they did with their faith. They believed this would help them manage their finances wisely and strengthen their bond.

One evening, Anne shared a verse she had read in Matthew 6:21: "For where your treasure is, there your heart will be also." She explained how their money dates were an embodiment of this verse. Their hearts were united in love and purpose as they discussed their financial priorities.

The couple's treasure was material possessions and shared goals and dreams. They knew that by working together, their hearts would remain connected through the sunny days and the storms of life.

Over the years, Peter and Anne's tradition of regular money dates became a cornerstone of their relationship. It wasn't just about money and building a solid foundation for their life together. Their faith, the biblical wisdom they drew upon, and their unwavering commitment to each other made their love a true testament to what could be achieved when two hearts are united in faith and finance.

Benefits of regular money dates.

1.   Strengthening Communication and Trust: Effective communication and trust are at the heart of any strong relationship. Money dates provide a dedicated space to discuss financial matters openly and honestly. You can share your financial goals, concerns, and dreams without judgment or tension. This open dialogue strengthens your connection, making trusting and supporting each other in all aspects of life more manageable.

2.   Setting Financial Goals Together: Money dates allow you and your partner to set financial goals together. Whether saving for a dream vacation, buying a home, or preparing for future

expenses, these dates help align your aspirations. When you both work towards common financial objectives, your unity grows stronger.

3.   Avoiding Financial Conflict: Money can often be a source of tension in relationships, but regular money dates can help you avoid these conflicts. By addressing financial concerns proactively, you can prevent misunderstandings and disagreements that might otherwise fester. This proactive approach is a testament to your commitment to one another's well-being.

4.   Building Financial Literacy: Biblical financial literacy is a valuable skill, and by searching the Scriptures together and discussing your finances regularly, you and your partner can learn and grow together. You can explore investment opportunities, budgeting techniques, and strategies for managing debt. These discussions empower you to make informed financial decisions, just as scripture encourages us to seek wisdom and understanding.

5.   Ensuring Equal Contribution: In the spirit of fairness and responsibility, money dates allow you to ensure that both partners contribute to the household's financial well-being. This aligns with biblical principles that emphasise providing for your own family. These dates help you find equitable ways to share the financial load and support each other.

Biblical guidance for the date

Here are five Biblical principles to guide regular money dates as a couple

1.   Transparency and Honesty: Open and honest communication is foundational. Be transparent about your financial situation, including income, expenses, debts, and financial goals. Proverbs 11:3 emphasises the importance of

honesty: "The integrity of the upright guides them, but the unfaithful are destroyed by their duplicity."

2.   Unity and Mutual Decision-Making: Approach financial matters as a team. Make financial decisions together, ensuring both partners have a say in budgeting, spending, and savings. This reflects the principle of unity emphasised in Genesis 2:24: "That is why a man leaves his father and mother and is united to his wife, and they become one flesh."

3.   Planning and Stewardship: Create a budget and financial plan during your money dates. Proverbs 21:5 highlights the importance of planning: "The plans of the diligent lead to profit as surely as haste leads to poverty." Be diligent stewards of your resources.

4.   Prayer and Seeking God's Guidance: Seek God's guidance in your financial decisions. Turn to prayer during your money dates, asking for wisdom and discernment. James 1:5 encourages seeking divine wisdom: "If any of you lacks wisdom, you should ask God, who gives generously to all without finding fault, and it will be given to you."

5.   Contentment and Gratitude: Cultivate contentment with what you have and express gratitude for God's blessings. 1 Timothy 6:6 reminds us: "But godliness with contentment is great gain." A thankful and content attitude can help reduce financial stress during money dates.

Regular money dates can be a huge blessing for your relationship. They foster communication, trust, and unity. Money dates help you make wise financial decisions that benefit your partnership and your future.

Consider incorporating regular money dates into your calendar. By doing so, you're strengthening your financial foundation and nurturing a love that grows, prospers, and withstands the tests of time.

Maintaining Financial Transparency

As a vital aspect of daily life, money inevitably finds its way into the heart of a marriage. It can be a source of joy and prosperity but also a breeding ground for disputes and mistrust. In navigating the financial journey as a couple, maintaining financial transparency is a cornerstone of building a harmonious relationship that thrives on trust and collaboration. Maintaining transparency in financial matters is essential for a strong and resilient marriage.

The Role of Ongoing Communication
Effective communication is the lifeblood of any marriage, and this principle holds even more significance when it comes to finances. Money often stirs emotions, whether it's the exhilaration of a financial win or the frustration of budget constraints. Thus, ongoing communication is essential for understanding each other's perspectives and navigating the financial landscape as a team.

Understanding Financial Goals: Regular conversations about financial goals are crucial. These discussions involve short-term objectives like saving for a holiday and long-term aspirations like retirement planning and children's education. By sharing these goals openly, couples can align their visions and work together to achieve them.

Setting time aside each month to discuss financial goals creates a shared vision and motivation to work toward these goals together.

Budgeting Together: Collaborative budgeting is an excellent practice. It ensures that both partners are aware of the financial status and promotes unity in decision-making. Establishing a monthly budget, tracking expenses, and reviewing it together can be a powerful tool for managing household finances.

This shared effort allows a couple to make informed decisions about spending and saving, promoting financial stability and a sense of togetherness.

Dealing with Financial Challenges: Life is full of unexpected financial challenges. Whether it's an unexpected medical expense, car repairs or a job loss, discussing these challenges openly and finding solutions as a couple can alleviate stress and strengthen the partnership.

An open dialogue in times of financial difficulty reinforces a partnership and promotes problem-solving skills.

Celebrating Financial Wins: On the flip side, celebrating financial wins is equally essential. Whether it's a job promotion, a successful investment, or reaching a savings milestone, recognising and celebrating these achievements together can foster positivity and shared success. By celebrating financial wins, a couple reinforces the idea that they are on this journey together through both challenges and triumphs.

Pray Together for Stronger Family Bonds

Prayer forms the cornerstone of family unity. It's the bedrock of a Christian home, fostering a deep connection that weathers the storms of life. Families that pray together forge unbreakable bonds, enhance communication, safeguard against external challenges, and nurture emotional resilience.

Within the sacred space of prayer, families can release their burdens, fears, and most profound feelings, strengthening their understanding of each other's fears, needs, and dreams. Additionally, prayer offers comfort during times of depression and anxiety and when facing the spectre of illnesses by providing a platform to discuss concerns and entrust them to God.

Is prayer a cherished practice in your family? Communicating with God is a powerful tool that enhances your household's happiness and resilience. As parents and caregivers, prayer rejuvenates tired spirits, offering wisdom and encouragement in times of frustration. It also instils in our children a deep awareness of our dependency on God, cultivating a special place for Him in our hearts.

Moreover, prayer reinforces the love bonds between partners, parents, and children. When family members intercede for one another, it deepens their appreciation and value for each other. Prayer also nurtures a sense of empathy for those beyond their own lives.

Look for opportunities to pray together as a family, starting with giving thanks during mealtime. Encourage your children to take turns leading prayers at the table. Bedtime is a tender moment for family members to listen to each other's prayers. Remember, no day should conclude without turning to God.

Don't forget the significant occasions such as times of illness or grief, when crucial family decisions loom, the outset of road trips, and during birthdays, celebrations, and anniversaries. Let your imagination guide you to discover even more opportunities for prayer. Never let busyness overshadow the profound strength that prayer can bring to your family.

The Catholic priest Patrick Peyton famously said, "The family who prays together stays together." [2]

Listening

Refining your listening skills is one of the most significant strides you can take in enhancing your communication. James 1:19-20 wisely advises, "Everyone should be quick to listen, slow to speak, and slow to become angry, for man's anger does not bring about the righteous life God desires." Giving undivided attention is essential to create an environment where your spouse feels free to confide in you, albeit it requires effort.

Maintaining unwavering eye contact may feel uncomfortable, and the urge to leap in with a quick solution can be challenging to resist, particularly for husbands who are often inclined to fix problems. However, respectful listening is the linchpin for comprehending your spouse's emotions and needs.

When your partner genuinely listens to you, you experience a sense of being cared for and understood, forming the bedrock for collaborative problem-solving. Many couples talk past each other when discussing financial matters, but only a few engage in conversations, enabling both partners to unveil their true sentiments safely.

Numerous conflicts arise from misconstrued assumptions about each other's intentions, making it imperative to ask as many questions as necessary to foster clarity. The simple yet potent question, "How can I support and assist you in handling this?" conveys your care and willingness to be of help. It signifies a desire to collaborate and strengthens the foundation of a harmonious partnership.

Cultivating Thankfulness

Incorporating gratitude into your relationship is closely related to offering encouragement. These five words hold immense significance:

"Unexpressed gratitude feels like ingratitude!"

Imagine a mother toiling for hours to prepare a birthday meal, only for her family to devour it in what seems like mere seconds. Though they are genuinely grateful for the meal, their failure to express it leaves her feeling unappreciated and taken for granted.

One of the most nourishing actions you can take for your marriage is to voice your authentic gratitude to your partner regularly. Thank them for their dedication to earning a living, affirm their wise financial decisions, and honour their generosity.

Philippians 4:8 captures this beautifully: "Whatever is true, whatever is noble, whatever is right, whatever is pure, whatever is lovely, whatever is admirable—if anything is excellent or praiseworthy—think about such things."

Take the time to write down what you appreciate about your partner, and remember to include financial aspects. Then, share these sentiments with each other and in prayer to God. This simple practice could revolutionise your marriage and your approach to finances.

Aligning Expectations for a Stronger Marriage

The merging of fiscal perspectives within a matrimonial bond can be a beacon of unity or a source of strain. Establishing a harmonious alignment of financial expectations is an indispensable cornerstone for fostering a resilient and enduring partnership.

Misunderstandings can often sow seeds of discord in a marriage, and a frequent culprit behind these issues is unmet and often unspoken expectations. It's a collaborative effort to shape misunderstandings!

Marital expectations encompass various domains, spanning from physical intimacy to household duties. Questions like, "Who's responsible for cooking?" or "Who should organise the party?" invariably emerge. When these inquiries are made with respect and openness, they delineate roles and responsibilities in the marriage. Conversely, when one spouse assumes the other's role without first discussing their expectations and arriving at a shared understanding, the household harmony can disintegrate, giving way to resentment and pain.

It's essential to understand that often, the problem doesn't lie with the other person but instead mirrors the disparities within us. To navigate these misunderstandings more effectively, it's crucial to acknowledge that your expectations are profoundly influenced by your upbringing, which might not be identical to your spouse's influences. The key is to find common ground.

Most couples enter marriage with positive expectations about their partner and their shared future, a mindset that fosters positive interactions and feelings. However, excessively high expectations can be challenging to satisfy, potentially leading to recurring disappointments, which, in turn, can diminish motivation to nurture the relationship further.

Expectations become problematic when they dictate our emotional responses, often manifesting as "shoulds" and "wishes." Conversing openly about these expectations and comparing them with reality effectively improves communication and avert conflicts.

Allow partners room to articulate their financial expectations, fears, and long-term goals. This exchange builds a foundation of trust, enabling both parties to comprehend each other's perspectives and collectively chart a financial course that resonates with their shared ambitions.

Aligning financial expectations in a marriage necessitates a blend of empathy, communication, and mutual respect. It's an ongoing journey rather than a destination—a continuous process of understanding, compromise, and shared decision-making.

Chapter 5. Preparing to marry

Jennifer and Jack eagerly anticipated their upcoming wedding. Amidst the excitement, a cloud of apprehension loomed over their heads. Their shared dreams often collided with the daunting financial realities.

An aspiring graphic designer, Jennifer poured her heart into her work but had unpredictable income. Jack, an ambitious software developer, revelled in his career's potential but was equally uncertain about stability in the light of a possible takeover.

As they meticulously planned their wedding, the cost of their dream celebration jolted them into thinking about the financial consequences. Each element they longed for seemed to bear a weighty price tag. Their aspirations for a dream event were tugged between desire and prudence.

Sitting across from each other one evening, they engaged in a heartfelt conversation. Jack confessed his concerns about the unpredictability of his career and the responsibility of providing for their future family. Jennifer, equally burdened, expressed her fears about the fluctuating nature of her work and the financial strain of their aspirations.

Their apprehensions were not merely about the wedding; they extended to their life beyond. The pressure of joining their lives and finances, managing debts, merging accounts, and navigating the intricacies of joint financial decisions weighed heavily on their hearts.

United in their determination, Jennifer and Jack sought guidance and explored strategies to secure their future together. As they immersed themselves in conversations about budgets, financial goals, and shared aspirations, a profound unity began to flourish. Their apprehension transformed into a source of motivation to build a stable foundation for their impending marriage. They joined a Compass small group to discover Biblical principles for marriage.

Their journey was no longer solely about planning a wedding; it became a testament to their unwavering commitment to weather financial storms together, hand in hand, promising a future built on trust, resilience, and shared dreams.

Financial implications of getting married.

Entering marriage is a union of hearts and a merger of financial lives. The financial implications of getting married encompass various aspects, from immediate changes in budgeting to long-term considerations like investments and estate planning. Let's delve into the critical financial implications couples should be aware of as they embark on this significant journey.

1. **Income and Expenses:** Combining incomes may lead to different tax implications and changes in the overall household budget. Restructuring expenses and savings is essential in line with this new financial reality.

2.   **Debt Responsibility:** Marriage may entail sharing responsibility for each other's debts, which can influence credit scores and future financial decisions.

3.   **Health Insurance and Benefits:** Couples might benefit from reviewing and potentially merging health insurance and other employee benefits, considering which plan best suits their joint needs.

4.   **Investments and Savings:** Joint financial goals and investment strategies might need adjustment to align with shared aspirations. Planning for long-term financial security becomes paramount.

5.   **Tax Filing:** Married couples can file taxes jointly or separately, each with implications for deductions, credits, and overall tax liability.

6.   **Legal Rights and Obligations:** Marriage confers legal rights and obligations, including property rights, spousal support, and decision-making authority in case of incapacitation.

7.   **Financial Compatibility:** Aligning financial values and attitudes is crucial for a harmonious financial future. Discussing money matters openly and honestly is key.

8.   **Communication and Compromise:** Financial decisions often require compromise and open communication to balance individual priorities and joint financial goals.

Understanding these financial implications can help couples navigate the financial landscape of marriage more effectively. Communication, planning, and occasionally seeking professional advice can significantly aid in managing the financial aspects of this beautiful journey together.

Biblical financial education

Studying the Bible's teachings on managing money before marriage is particularly essential as it lays the groundwork for financial unity and shared values right from the onset of the union. Before marriage, couples can align their perspectives, understand each other's economic backgrounds, and establish a framework for handling money matters together.

Before entering into marriage, is an ideal time to discuss and understand each other's attitudes towards money, debts, spending habits, and long-term financial aspirations. This early understanding forms the basis for aligning financial goals and strategies as a couple.

Engaging with the Bible's teachings on money management before marriage can help prevent conflicts and financial value discrepancies. This proactive approach enables couples to address these differences early on, reducing the likelihood of misunderstandings and disagreements in the future.

This pre-marriage study and discussion about financial principles allow couples to develop shared values and principles regarding money. This shared understanding becomes the basis for joint decision-making and financial planning throughout their married life, ensuring a harmonious approach to managing money as a couple.

You're engaged, and now you're preparing for the big day. There are a thousand things on your mind. Wedding dress. Invitations. A cake. A photographer. The list goes on and on.

What about your finances? If you're a typical single, you do your best to manage your finances and understand how much is entering and exiting your bank account. But now you're getting married. What should change?

Engaged couples preparing for marriage often face distinct financial challenges as they transition from individual finances to a joint financial journey. Some unique challenges include:

Merging Financial Practices: Couples entering marriage bring their financial habits and practices. Bridging these distinct budgeting, spending, and saving approaches can be challenging. Finding a harmonious way to manage finances while respecting each other's perspectives becomes crucial. Before marriage, it's important not to assume the privileges and responsibilities of a married couple.

Merging finances before tying the knot can create a significant and messy situation, mainly if a breakup occurs. When relationships come to an end, tensions are already heightened. Adding merged finances to this situation only complicates matters further. Merge accounts only after marriage!

Combining finances reduces the number of accounts to manage and allows a couple to reframe the idea of separate ownership, shifting from "mine" and "yours" to a collective "ours." This method replaces individualistic mindsets with a unified approach to shared resources.

Different Financial Backgrounds: Varying financial backgrounds, including debts, assets, and spending patterns, can pose challenges. Managing these differences in income, savings, and financial priorities requires open and honest discussions to align goals and strategies.

Wedding Expenses: The financial strain of wedding expenses can be significant. Balancing the desire for a beautiful ceremony with the practicality of staying within budget tests the couple's financial planning skills. Overspending on the wedding can affect the early stages of the marriage and set a precedent for future financial decisions.

Setting Joint Financial Goals: Establishing common financial goals requires understanding and compromise. Differing priorities and aspirations need adjustment to find a shared vision for the future. Agreeing on saving strategies, investment choices, and long-term plans is crucial.

Legal and Tax Implications: Understanding the legal and tax implications of marriage is vital. Jointly filing taxes, sharing responsibility for debts, and determining property rights can be complex. Seeking professional advice to navigate these legal and financial intricacies becomes essential.

Family Expectations and Support: Family expectations and support can also influence financial decisions. Balancing expectations while making choices that align with the couple's financial well-being might pose a challenge.

Navigating these unique financial challenges requires open communication, mutual respect, and a willingness to compromise. Establishing a solid financial foundation involves managing the immediate financial aspects and creating a plan for the future that reflects the values and aspirations of the couple in their journey together.

Pre-nuptial agreements

John and Susanne, a devoted Christian couple, were in deep contemplation one evening. They were planning their upcoming wedding, and the topic of a prenuptial agreement had surfaced. It was a conversation that required careful consideration and prayer.

John broke the silence as they sat together over dinner. "Susanne, I've been thinking about the idea of a prenuptial agreement," he admitted. "I want to discuss it with you."
Susanne nodded thoughtfully. She understood that this was a significant step that warranted earnest deliberation. "I'm glad you brought it up, John. We should make this decision together, guided

by our faith."
Both John and Susanne believed that their faith in God was the cornerstone of their relationship. They questioned whether a prenuptial agreement might imply a lack of trust in God's plan for their marriage. On the practical side, they acknowledged that a prenuptial agreement could offer financial protection, particularly in unforeseen circumstances. They discussed the importance of ensuring their financial futures were secure.

John and Susanne recognised that their families might have strong opinions on the matter. They considered how their loved ones would perceive their decision and its impact on family dynamics. They both valued open communication. They agreed that discussing the prenuptial agreement allowed them to be transparent about their financial expectations, obligations, and any concerns they might have.

Their faith played a significant role in their decision-making process. They turned to biblical principles about marriage, understanding that the Bible encourages spouses to honour and care for each other's well-being.

The Bible does not explicitly address prenuptial agreements, as they are a modern legal concept. However, we can draw insights from biblical principles that help inform a Christian perspective on prenuptial agreements.

First and foremost, it's essential to understand that God designed marriage to be a lifelong commitment intended to last as long as both spouses are alive. When two Christian individuals enter into matrimony, it should be with a firm belief that divorce is not an option.

God's creation of Eve from Adam's rib symbolises the purpose of the husband-and-wife relationship. They are joined as one flesh, signifying an inseparable bond. This unity should discourage any thoughts of separation. Divorce was only permitted in the Old Testament because of the people's insistence and hardness of heart (Matthew 19:8). God, who never changes, disapproves of divorce (Malachi 2:16).

The love described in 1 Corinthians 13 should ideally render prenuptial agreements unnecessary. Biblical love, as outlined in this chapter, is a conscious decision to prioritise the best interests of others, just as God always seeks our best. This love is patient, kind, unselfish, forgiving, and enduring, making prenuptial agreements seem out of place in a Christian marriage.

Ephesians 5 guides the roles of husbands and wives in marriage. Husbands are called to love their wives sacrificially, mirroring Christ's love for the church. Wives are encouraged to honour their husbands and submit to their leadership. Just as Christ never leaves us, a husband should remain committed to his wife. These principles emphasise the permanence of the union and the importance of selflessness, traits that prenuptial agreements might cast doubt upon.

For two committed Christian individuals, prenuptial agreements may seem unnecessary. While both spouses may fall short and sin, love is meant to cover many sins (1 Peter 4:8). God calls us to forgive each other as He forgives us, and prenuptial agreements essentially plan for the opposite. If a husband and wife genuinely become one, the lines between "yours" and "mine" should fade or at least significantly blur.

Many consider prenuptial agreements a practical step in today's society, but we should remember that God's ways often differ from the world's. The Bible does not support the idea that engaged Christian couples should create a "just in case of divorce, you can't take my possessions" agreement. Instead, it encourages faith, trust, and love in the sacred bond of marriage.

If a prenuptial agreement is considered, it should be drafted in a fair and just manner that respects both partners' rights and interests. Unfair or one-sided agreements may not align with biblical principles of justice and fairness.

It's essential to ensure that any prenuptial agreement is legally sound and complies with the laws of the land. Christians are encouraged to follow the laws of the land (Romans 13:1-2).

A prenuptial agreement, which is increasingly common among blended families, may be necessary to clarify which assets will be jointly owned and which will be kept separate – and, more importantly, how your money will be divided should the marriage dissolve.

Ultimately, the view on prenuptial agreements in Christianity may vary among individuals and denominations. Some may see them as a practical way to address financial matters, while others may view them as contrary to the spirit of trust and commitment in marriage.
It's important for couples to engage in open and honest discussions about financial matters, including the possibility of a prenuptial agreement, and to seek guidance from their church or a trusted spiritual advisor when making decisions that impact their marriage.

Wedding

The financial implications of wise spending on a wedding reverberate far beyond the ceremony itself. Making prudent financial decisions impacts the wedding day and sets the tone for a couple's financial future.

A wedding is a beautiful milestone, but overspending on this single event can create unnecessary financial strain. Opting for wise spending involves setting a realistic budget that aligns with the couple's financial situation. This prudent approach allows for a celebration that mirrors their values and priorities without burdening them with long-term debt.

Moreover, the funds allocated for the wedding can be strategically diverted towards more substantial investments for the future, such as a down payment on a house, creating an emergency fund, or starting a joint investment portfolio. This intelligent allocation of resources ensures that the couple begins their journey with financial stability rather than a weighty financial hangover.

Also, making cost-effective wedding choices doesn't diminish its significance or beauty. Creativity in planning, prioritising elements that hold sentimental value, and exploring affordable yet elegant alternatives can create a memorable and heartfelt celebration.

In essence, wise spending on a wedding ensures a beautiful ceremony within financial means and sets the stage for a financially secure future. It's about celebrating the beginning of a life together while making prudent financial decisions that pave the way for a stable and prosperous journey ahead.

Planning a wedding.

When outlining the budget, identify and prioritise the most significant elements for you both. Whether it's the church, venue, food, photography, or specific details, allocate a larger portion of the budget to these critical areas while being open to adjustments in less vital aspects.

Flexibility in terms of the wedding date and venue can significantly impact costs. Consider choosing off-peak seasons or less popular days for weddings. This approach can substantially reduce venue expenses, offering potential savings.

Managing the guest list is crucial in keeping costs in check. Limiting the number of guests reduces catering and venue expenses. Consider inviting only close friends and family to ensure a more intimate celebration.

Leverage your creativity and consider do-it-yourself projects to personalise decorations, invitations, or party favours.

DIY projects can add a personal touch while saving significant money.

Choose digital invitations instead of traditional printed ones. Not only does this save money, but it also aligns with eco-friendly practices, reducing the environmental impact.

Exploring more affordable dress options, considering attire rental, or opting for a simpler ensemble can yield substantial savings on wedding attire. For the groom, renting a suit can be a cost-effective alternative.

Engage with local vendors and negotiate prices. Sometimes, local businesses offer competitive rates compared to larger companies, providing quality services within your budget.

Streamlining the menu or choosing buffet-style dining can reduce catering costs without compromising on the quality of the food. Similarly, finding ways to simplify and economise other aspects of the celebration can lead to significant savings.

Regularly review and adjust the budget throughout the planning process. Keeping a close eye on expenses helps you stay on track and make necessary adjustments as needed. The goal is to avoid accumulating unnecessary debt for a one-day celebration and start your married life financially stable.

Chapter 6: Maintaining Financial Harmony

This chapter dives deeper into the critical aspect of communication and its impact on financial harmony within marriage. It addresses the need for open and honest dialogue, strategies for dealing with financial conflicts, and how personal financial values and beliefs shape marital money discussions.

The foundation for financial harmony within a marriage is built upon biblical principles that advocate honesty, transparency, and accountability in financial matters. These principles not only guide couples in managing money but also contribute to the overall health and unity of the relationship.

Honesty

Honesty is a cornerstone of the biblical approach to financial harmony. Ephesians 4:25 instructs us, "Therefore each of you must put off falsehood and speak truthfully to your neighbour, for we are all members of one body." This principle of speaking truth extends to the marriage relationship. Being honest about financial matters means discussing income, expenses, debts, and financial goals openly. It entails sharing both the successes and challenges in managing money.

Honesty in financial matters fosters trust and helps couples make informed decisions. It prevents misunderstandings and financial secrets that can lead to conflicts. Ultimately, it creates an environment where both spouses feel respected and valued, knowing they can openly express their financial concerns and aspirations.

Transparency

Transparency in financial matters goes hand in hand with honesty. It involves revealing all relevant financial information to one's spouse. Proverbs 21:5 states, "The plans of the diligent lead to profit as surely as haste leads to poverty." Transparency ensures both spouses know the household's financial plans, goals, and expenditures.

Openly sharing financial information allows couples to work together in creating a budget, setting financial goals, and making financial decisions. It eliminates the potential for misunderstandings and hidden financial surprises. Transparency helps foster a sense of unity in financial matters, as both spouses actively participate in shaping the family's financial future.

In their book, "The Complete Marriage Book", [i] Dr David Stoop and Dr Jan Stoop say, "There is an incredible vulnerability that comes when we give another person access to our finances. The reality is they can now hurt us very badly by taking or misusing the information we have given them. Prior to marriage, many of us had to answer only to ourselves. A major shift occurred as we began our married life. We are now accountable to each other. How do you react when someone limits you? This is where "iron sharpens iron" (see Proverbs 27:17) and the sparks begin to fly." [3]

Accountability

Accountability in financial matters within a marriage is a biblical principle that encourages spouses to hold each other responsible for their financial decisions. This entails a sense of submission to one another, as Ephesians 5:21 tells us, "submit to one another out of reverence for Christ." This principle encourages a sense of shared responsibility for financial choices.

If one partner makes a mistake or does something wrong, he or she should be honest about it. The other should be willing to share the load and seek restoration. "Brothers, if anyone is caught in any transgression, you who are spiritual should restore him in a spirit of gentleness. Keep watch on yourself, lest you too be tempted. Bear one another's burdens, and so fulfil the law of Christ." (Galatians 6:1,2)

Accountability in financial matters can take the form of regular financial discussions, joint decision-making, and shared responsibility for financial goals. It means that both spouses are actively involved in managing the family's finances and are accountable to each other. This accountability promotes financial harmony and strengthens the marital bond by fostering a sense of partnership and mutual support.

Building Trust

Sylvie and Bert, a once-trusting couple, struggled when trust began to waver in their financial relationship. It all began when Bert started making spontaneous purchases they hadn't agreed upon, which left Sylvie feeling betrayed and uncertain about their financial stability.

Sylvie's meticulously planned budgets and savings were in disarray, and she struggled to regain confidence in their shared financial decisions. Bert, recognising his missteps, felt remorseful for his actions but also felt judged for his financial choices.

The couple decided to address this issue head-on. They scheduled regular financial discussions and established clear boundaries for discretionary spending. With time, transparency, and a commitment to rebuilding trust, they began to repair their financial relationship. Bert learned to respect their agreed-upon financial boundaries, while Sylvie began to appreciate the importance of flexibility and compromise. Through open communication, they gradually regained the trust that had been temporarily strained.

Nurturing Trust in Your Marriage

Dishonesty with money can be incredibly detrimental to a marriage. Shockingly, over 50 per cent of couples engage in hidden spending or financial decisions, believing these secrets are harmless.[liii] However, they can prove fatal to the relationship.

The Lord calls for complete honesty. Leviticus 19:11 instructs us, "You shall not steal or deal falsely or lie to one another."

Trust is the lifeblood of a successful marriage. It is as vital as oxygen, and a "Trust Account" analogy can be helpful. Like a bank account, you can make deposits and withdrawals. Deposits are made through open communication, honesty, and involving your spouse in financial decisions. Withdrawals, on the other hand, result from dishonesty, disregarding your spouse's financial input, and failing to use money to benefit your partner.

Earning trust takes time and dedication; there are no shortcuts. Take as much care with your Trust Account as you would with your Savings Account!

Building your trust account

Full Disclosure: Disclosing all financial details to your spouse is essential. This includes income, debts, assets, and spending habits. Being fully transparent fosters trust and eliminates potential surprises down the road.

Imagine Sylvie has credit card debt that she hasn't shared with Bert. As the debt accumulates, she becomes increasingly stressed and worried about how Bert will react when he finds out. Eventually, she decides to come clean and tells Bert about the debt. While he's initially surprised, he appreciates her honesty. Together, they work on a plan to pay down the debt, and their trust deepens as they face the challenge as a team.

No Hidden Agendas: Financial discussions should be void of hidden agendas. Working together and making financial decisions that benefit the marriage rather than pursuing individual interests is essential.

One day, Bert suggests investing a substantial portion of their savings in a business opportunity he's excited about without discussing it with Sylvie first. She feels blindsided and concerned about the potential risks. This incident leads to a conversation where they agree to consider each other's input and collectively make financial decisions. This commitment to no hidden agendas fosters a sense of unity in their financial choices.

Equal Partnership: Financial decisions should ideally be made jointly. This promotes a sense of equality and shared responsibility. Both partners should have a say in major financial choices, from investments to significant expenses.

In their earlier years of marriage, Sylvie and Bert occasionally found themselves in disputes over financial decisions. Realising this was causing strain in their relationship, they approached their finances as an equal partnership. They began holding regular financial meetings to discuss important decisions, ensuring their voices were heard. This shift towards equality in financial matters improved their communication and decision-making, strengthening their bond.

Accountability: Transparency leads to accountability. When both partners can access and understand the family's financial information, they can hold each other accountable for responsible financial behaviour.

Bert tends to overspend on his hobbies, sometimes causing financial strain. However, he knows Sylvie knows their budget and observes their financial transactions. This knowledge alone encourages him to be more accountable for his spending, reducing impulsive purchases and ensuring financial responsibility.

Planning for the Future: Planning for the future is a collective effort. When trust is present in a marriage, long-term financial planning becomes an exciting journey toward shared goals. This includes planning for retirement, saving for children's education, and building generational wealth.

Having built trust and transparency in their financial relationship, Sylvie and Bert embark on a journey to plan for their future. They set aside time to discuss their retirement goals, establish a college fund for their children, and explore investment opportunities. By openly discussing their financial future, they create a roadmap that excites them and strengthens their bond as they work together towards their dreams.

Overcoming Financial Challenges Together: The test of trust and collaboration in financial matters often comes during tough times. Whether facing debt, job loss, or financial setbacks, a robust and transparent partnership allows couples to confront these challenges together and emerge stronger on the other side.

When Sylvie and Bert encountered financial setbacks due to unexpected medical bills, they rallied together to find solutions rather than pointing fingers or blaming each other. They review their budget regularly, explore financial assistance options, and provide emotional support to one another. This experience helps them overcome the challenge and deepens their trust and collaboration as they emerge from it stronger as a couple.

In a marriage, maintaining financial transparency goes beyond merely sharing bank statements; it involves creating an environment of trust, understanding, and collaboration. When couples communicate openly, build trust, and work together toward shared financial goals, they set the stage for a prosperous and harmonious financial future. Money may be a part of the equation, but the heart of the matter is the strength and unity of the partnership itself. By actively practising financial transparency, communication, and trust-building, couples can forge a path towards lasting financial harmony, enriching their relationship.

Be an encouragement

One of the most important ways to bless your spouse is to be an encourager. Let's face it: life can be hard. Your spouse may have low self-esteem and not realise God has gifted them with unique abilities.

So, be a cheerleader for your spouse because it's a proper biblical priority. The Bible tells us, "Let us encourage one another." (Hebrews 10:25) and "encourage one another and build each other up." (1 Thessalonians 5:11)

Being an encourager isn't just a nice thing; it's an essential nutrient that keeps loving relationships growing!

Bert had been working hard to repair the damage he had caused earlier in their marriage. Sylvie explained, "When the person that means the most to you is always finding fault, it is incredibly painful. I didn't feel I had anything to contribute to our finances. But now that Bert encourages me, I feel loved and energised to help improve our finances."

Spend to enrich your partner.

During the early years of our marriage, I admit I was more focused on spending in ways that catered to my desires, often neglecting my wife's wishes. It took me some time to realise the profound wisdom of Philippians 2:3-4 when applied to marriage: "Do nothing out of selfish ambition or vain conceit, but in humility consider others better than yourselves. Each of you should look not only to your own interests but also to the interests of others."

As I deepened my relationship with Christ, a fundamental shift occurred in my perspective. The pivotal question became, "How can I use our financial resources to be a source of joy and blessing to my wife, Didie?" She always sought ways to bless me by buying what I needed.

God's call for us to bless one another extends to the bonds between husbands and wives. "To sum up, all of you be harmonious, sympathetic, brotherly, kind-hearted, and humble in spirit; not returning evil for evil or insult for insult, but giving a blessing instead; for you were called for the very purpose that you might inherit a blessing" (1 Peter 3:8-9).

Embracing the mindset of wanting to enrich your partner's life through your spending decisions often leads to a remarkable revelation: the joy derived from buying something for them surpasses the satisfaction of purchasing something for yourself. It's a tangible demonstration of what Jesus conveyed in Acts 20:35: "It is more blessed to give than to receive."

Combining Earnings in Marriage

In a world where financial independence is highly emphasised, the concept of pooling earnings in marriage can seem counterintuitive to some. However, from a Biblical standpoint, combining resources within a marriage is rooted in wisdom and unity.

Julia and Mark had been happily married for three years. They loved each other deeply but had a fundamental difference regarding their finances. They kept their incomes separate and maintained individual accounts. Initially, this financial independence seemed like a healthy choice, allowing them to spend their money as they pleased. However, as time passed, problems began to arise.

A diligent saver, Julia meticulously budgeted her income and built a robust savings account. She had dreams of homeownership and financial security. Mark, on the other hand, was a free spender. He enjoyed dining at expensive restaurants and splurging on gadgets. Arguments about money became a regular occurrence. Julia felt that Mark's spending was jeopardising their financial future, while Mark believed Julia's frugality stifled his freedom.

Over time, their separate finances created a lack of transparency and trust in their relationship. They started to hide purchases from each other, leading to mistrust and secrecy. Their problems escalated when they decided to purchase a car. Julia wanted to use her savings for a down payment, while Mark was reluctant to part with his cash. The disagreements intensified, and they were no closer to a resolution. Their love began to wane under the weight of financial strain. They realised that their separate accounts were causing more harm than good.

After seeking advice from a financial counsellor, they pooled their incomes and created a shared account for all household expenses. It wasn't an easy transition, but they found it immensely liberating.

Pooling their income allowed for better financial transparency and trust. They set common goals and budget together, learning to compromise on spending habits.

Their relationship began to flourish once more. They bought their dream car together, and the mutual trust and openness improved their communication and overall happiness."

Julia and Mark discovered that love and money could coexist harmoniously. By pooling their income, they created a stronger, more resilient partnership, proving that sometimes, financial togetherness can strengthen the bonds of love.

Pooling earnings in marriage reflects the profound biblical principles of unity, mutual accountability, selflessness, trust, and support for God's work. It is a way for couples to strengthen their bond and demonstrate their commitment to living out God's plan for marriage. By working together in this manner, they can experience the blessings of a truly harmonious and God-honoring partnership.

Let's explore this harmonious approach to managing finances in marriage.

One Flesh, One Money

Genesis 2:24 tells us, "That is why a man leaves his father and mother and is united to his wife, and they become one flesh." This profound verse emphasises the unity that marriage brings. In a marriage, the union goes far beyond physical and emotional; it also extends to financial matters.

When a husband and wife choose to pool their earnings, they essentially put into practice the concept of becoming "one flesh" in all aspects of life, including their finances. This unity creates a sense of togetherness and shared responsibility, a fundamental aspect of a successful and God-honoring marriage.

Mutual Accountability

Paul reminds Timothy to ensure he will be "holding on to faith and a good conscience, which some have rejected and so have suffered shipwreck with regard to the faith." (1 Timothy 1:19) Accountability can help us maintain a clear conscience. When couples pool their earnings, they are accountable to one another for their financial decisions.

Pooling earnings allows both spouses to have a say in the family's financial choices, ensuring they work together to manage resources wisely. This shared accountability can help prevent excessive debt and promote responsible financial stewardship.

Meeting Each Other's Needs

Philippians 2:4 teaches us, "Not looking to your interests but each of you to the interests of the others." In marriage, it's essential to prioritise each other's needs and well-being. Combining earnings allows couples to meet the needs of both partners and their families.

Pooling earnings enables couples to share the financial burdens and blessings that come their way. This approach reflects a commitment to selflessness and mutual support, central to the Christian faith.

Strengthening Trust and Transparency

Proverbs 11:3 states, "The integrity of the upright guides them, but the unfaithful are destroyed by their duplicity." Honesty and transparency are vital in a godly marriage. Pooling earnings fosters trust and open communication, encouraging both spouses to be transparent about their financial situation.

By sharing their financial lives, couples can collaborate to make informed decisions, set mutual financial goals, and ensure their resources are used wisely. This strengthens their relationship and aligns with biblical principles of integrity and trust.

Give room for some "Me" Money.

Allocating a specific amount of "me money" to each partner can reduce recurring money-related conflicts. Many arguments stem from individual expenses paid from a shared account, so it's wise to establish a personal spending budget for each partner to use at their discretion. After all, you've put in the hard work to earn your money, and you should never feel like you need approval before making non-major purchases.

However, it's crucial to emphasise that having individual discretionary spending accounts should not be a pretext for keeping financial secrets from your partner. Concealing financial matters involving credit card bills or new purchases can harm any relationship and hinder open and honest communication. If you cannot openly discuss your purchases and expenditures because you fear your partner's disapproval, it's an issue that should be addressed and resolved together.

When Spending Habits Collide

Marriage is a union of two individuals with distinct backgrounds, personalities, and life experiences. These differences often manifest in various aspects of life, including spending habits. Some partners may be savers, carefully budgeting and planning expenses, while others are natural spenders, enjoying life's pleasures without much thought for tomorrow. These differences can lead to financial tension within a marriage.

A marriage, once filled with love, can become a battlefield. Open conversations give way to silence and avoidance, causing love and communication to wither as resentment grows.

James lost his job, and their paltry savings couldn't cushion the blow. Their financial crisis was a turning point. To make ends meet, they reluctantly sold some cherished possessions. Amid the turmoil, they realised their silence had inflicted more harm. Failure to communicate had endangered their marriage. Instead of allowing financial perspectives to drive them apart, they should have addressed these differences together.

In their quest for change, they sought marriage counselling. Their counsellor urged openness, sharing fears and dreams, and creating a financial plan accommodating both spending habits. As they talked, they discovered that their differences could complement each other. Laura's discipline curbed James's impulsiveness, while James's spontaneity enriched Laura's life.

With newfound understanding and a commitment to open dialogue, they rebuilt their financial future and, more importantly, their relationship. Their differences remained, but they had learned to appreciate and balance them.

Laura and James realised it wasn't their spending habits at fault but their inability to discuss and collaborate. They found that love could conquer even the most challenging financial hurdles through communication, understanding, and compromise.

Challenges of Different Spending Habits

Differences in spending habits can lead to several challenges in a marriage:

1. Conflict and Misunderstandings: Opposing spending habits can result in misunderstandings and arguments, with savers seeing spenders as irresponsible and spenders seeing savers as overly cautious.

2. Financial Stress: The financial stress created by clashing spending habits can jeopardise a couple's financial security and stability.

3. Mismatched Priorities: Disagreements over spending can reveal mismatched financial priorities, potentially leading to resentment and emotional distance.

Marriage brings together two individuals with unique perspectives and behaviours, including spending habits. The differences can be a source of tension, but a biblical perspective emphasises communication, mutual respect, and compromise to reconcile these disparities. By openly discussing their financial priorities and values, seeking wisdom and counsel, practising mutual submission, and creating shared financial goals, couples can navigate their differences in spending habits and build a robust and harmonious partnership.

Combatants or Companions?

In most couples, differences are not just common but practically guaranteed. One is a night owl, the other an early bird. One immerses in details, and the other sees the big picture. One gets lost in a paper bag, while the other always knows the way. One wants to invest, and the other is more inclined to spend.

These distinctions can lead to conflict, turning what drew you together into a battleground. It's a choice – do you become adversaries or companions? Remember, you were initially attracted to each other because of these differences, and trying to change someone's core personality is not the answer.

Opposites attract, and when you embrace your disparities as assets, you can discover that they bring fresh perspectives. When it comes to money, this diversity can be a powerful tool, offering a range of insights and contributing to wise decision-making. It's all about balance.

Money often reveals your unique money personality, and understanding these can be the first step in shaping your approach to finances. This understanding enables both partners to support each other, creating harmony in their financial decisions. Like in life, your responses to money are primarily influenced by your personality. So, by appreciating and working together with your differences, you can achieve a prosperous, balanced marriage.

Chapter 7: Handling financial conflicts

In a world that often prioritises material possessions and financial success, it's no surprise that money can be a source of tension in a marriage. Differences in spending habits, financial goals, and communication about money can lead to conflicts. These conflicts can challenge the principles of unity and stewardship that are important in a Christian marriage.

Fred and Angela possess contrasting approaches when it comes to managing their finances. Angela, the meticulous planner, meticulously structures their financial landscape. She's the one with detailed spreadsheets, a meticulously allocated budget and a clear roadmap for their financial future. Angela's foresight ensures stability and security, giving her a sense of assurance in uncertain times.

On the flip side, there's Fred, the consummate opportunist. He thrives on spontaneity, always on the lookout for the next big thing. His optimistic view of the world leads him to embrace risk and leap at unexpected opportunities. While Angela values security, Fred seeks excitement and instant gratification, often causing friction when their financial philosophies clash.

Their conflicting approaches spark debates about priorities, risk tolerance, and the balance between stability and adventure. Angela advocates for careful planning and building a solid foundation, while Fred champions seizing the moment and taking calculated risks for potential gains.

Yet, within this financial tug-of-war, Fred and Angela learn invaluable lessons from each other. Angela discovers the joy of spontaneity and the thrill of taking calculated risks, while Fred begins to appreciate the security and peace of mind that comes from careful planning.

In their journey of financial harmony, Fred and Angela gradually find a middle ground, blending their diverse perspectives to create a balanced approach that embraces both security and opportunity.

Marriage is a sacred union and a partnership that extends to all aspects of life, including finances. Financial conflicts are common in marriages; if left unaddressed, they can strain the bond between partners. In this blog article, we will explore how to resolve financial conflicts in marriage from a biblical perspective, drawing wisdom from the Scriptures."

Consequences of financial conflicts in marriage

Financial conflicts in marriage can have far-reaching consequences.

First and foremost, failing to work out financial conflicts can strain the very foundation of a marriage. Money matters often revolve around differing values, spending habits, and financial goals. Ignoring these issues can create a sense of mistrust and resentment between spouses. The Bible reminds us to be of one mind in marriage; financial disputes can hinder that unity. The

Apostle Paul asks believers in Philippi to "complete my joy by being of the same mind, having the same love, being in full accord and of one mind. Do nothing from selfish ambition or conceit, but in humility count others more significant than yourselves. Let each of you look not only to his own interests, but also to the interests of others." (Philippians 2:2-4)

Moreover, unresolved financial conflicts can lead to anxiety and stress. The burden of unpaid bills, mounting debt, or uncertainty about the future can weigh heavily on both partners. This stress can spill over into other aspects of life, affecting emotional and physical well-being, which is not what our Lord intended for His children.

Left unaddressed, financial conflicts may also lead to secrecy and dishonesty. Couples may start hiding their spending or financial decisions from each other. This undermines the transparency and open communication that are essential for a strong marriage. We're called to walk in the light and truth, not in shadows.

In extreme cases, financial conflicts can even lead to separation or divorce. It's heartbreaking to see marriages disintegrate because of disputes over money. Our faith encourages us to seek reconciliation and forgiveness, but if financial conflicts are allowed to fester, it can become increasingly difficult to heed these calls.

Remember that financial conflicts are opportunities for growth, understanding, and a deeper connection in your marriage.

Financial Infidelity: Finding Healing and Restoration

Financial infidelity is a deeply sensitive topic that can erode trust and intimacy within a marriage. While the concept of infidelity is typically associated with breaches of faithfulness in marital relationships, financial infidelity involves deceit or dishonesty regarding financial matters. The last true taboo in relationships is not sex - it's money.

I recently read a recent U.S. study called "Couples have their dirty little secrets", which indicated that as many as 80% of spouses admitted to secret shopping and 18% of married people indicated that they have a credit card that their partner has no idea exists. [4]

In addition, 34% said they feared that if their spouse found out the truth, they would ask for a divorce. Nearly half said they were hiding economic information from their husbands or wives because they didn't want to fight about it. [iii]

Amy and Mark had been married for ten years; they shared their dreams, laughter, and even the sorrow life sometimes brings. What they didn't share was their financial secrets.

One evening, as Mark paid their bills, he discovered a stack of credit card statements he'd never seen. The numbers were shocking. Amy had been hiding her credit card debt for years, charging luxuries they couldn't afford. The revelation was a bombshell. Mark felt deceived, betrayed, and deeply hurt. He confronted Amy about her financial infidelity, his voice trembling with a mix of anger and sadness. She confessed, tearfully admitting her mistakes. She explained that she wanted to maintain a particular lifestyle to avoid disappointing him.

Their once-loving marriage became marred by mistrust and arguments. The financial infidelity had torn a rift between them. Mark was left to bear the weight of debt he didn't know existed, and Amy grappled with guilt.

As they tried to repair the damage, they sought counselling and committed to transparency in their financial dealings. Mark forgave Amy, understanding that everyone makes mistakes. They devised a budget, worked together to pay the debt, and rekindled their love. It took time, but they rebuilt the trust that had been shattered.

Like a hidden crack in a dam, financial infidelity can eventually lead to a devastating rupture in a marriage. Financial infidelity has severe consequences for a marriage. It can erode trust, lead to arguments, and strain the emotional connection in a marriage. It can hinder financial stability and create a sense of betrayal, just as emotional infidelity does. Yet, the couple can rebuild the bond with humility, forgiveness, and a willingness to change.
Amy and Mark emerged from the ordeal with a stronger marriage, having learned that financial secrets have no place in a relationship built on trust and love.

"Financial infidelity can be as bad as sexual infidelity, in terms of the pain and destruction it causes." So, what is to be done about it? The Bible gives us clear indications. "Therefore each of you must put off falsehood and speak truthfully to your neighbour, for we are all members of one body." (Ephesians 4:25)
We risk becoming separated if we don't do our best to maintain unity in our decisions. "I therefore, a prisoner for the Lord, urge you to walk in a manner worthy of the calling to which you have been called, with all humility and gentleness, with patience, bearing with one another in love, eager to maintain the unity of the Spirit in the bond of peace." (Ephesians 4:1-3)

Hiding purchases and economic decisions from your spouse may be the beginning of the end. The reason? TRUST, a necessary ingredient for any relationship, is destroyed.

Causes of Financial Infidelity
Financial infidelity often stems from underlying issues within the marriage. These causes can include:

• Keeping secrets: One partner may make purchases and hide them from the other or hide financial decisions like making investments or supporting family members financially.

• Financial Lies: Lying about income or spending.

• Lack of Communication: Failure to discuss financial matters openly can lead to misunderstandings and secret financial activities.

• Financial Stress: Pressure to meet financial goals can drive some individuals to make desperate and secretive financial decisions.

• Differing Values: Misalignment in financial values and priorities can lead to hidden spending or saving.

• Individual Financial Baggage: Past financial experiences or traumas can influence financial behaviours.

• Different Money Personalities: Spouses may have differing attitudes and approaches to money. If these differences are not acknowledged and addressed, they can give rise to financial secrecy.

• Inadequate Financial Education: Lack of knowledge about managing money can lead to impulsive financial decisions, including accumulating debt without the other spouse's knowledge.

• Emotional Issues: Stress, unresolved conflicts, or emotional issues can trigger financial infidelity as a coping mechanism.

Moving Forward in Love and Forgiveness

Addressing money infidelity is a challenging journey, but it's essential for the health and longevity of a marriage. By following biblical principles of trust, honesty, communication, and forgiveness, couples can overcome the impact of financial betrayal and rebuild their relationship on a foundation of love and faith. Remember, God's grace and wisdom are always available to guide us through these challenging moments.

Money infidelity is a challenging issue that can erode trust, hinder communication, and strain the emotional bonds in a marriage. However, by applying biblical principles of trust, honesty, and forgiveness, couples can overcome the impact of financial betrayal and rebuild their relationship on a foundation of love and faith. The journey may be challenging, but with God's grace and guidance, it is possible to navigate the path to healing and restoration.

The Dynamics of Financial Control in Marriage

Financial control in marriage arises when one partner assumes the primary role in managing the finances. This control can manifest in budgeting, investments, and spending decisions, often driven by income disparities or perceived financial expertise.

Financial control within a marriage can manifest for various reasons, often stemming from individual beliefs, insecurities, or life experiences. Understanding these underlying factors can help address and prevent such issues. Here are some common reasons behind financial control in marriages:

"Anna and Tim had a love that once felt unshakable, but an insurmountable issue now marred their relationship. Tim had taken it upon himself to control how they used their money, which had sown the seeds of discontent.

At first, Tim's financial vigilance seemed like responsible stewardship. He managed the budget meticulously, determining what was allowed and what was not. Anna, initially accepting, soon felt the noose of control tightening. She yearned for the freedom to make her own financial choices, even if they weren't always perfect.

Tim's controlling nature began to erode their communication. He scrutinised every expense, questioned her purchases, and criticised her for deviating from his carefully crafted financial plan. Anna felt disempowered, unheard, and unloved.

Their love began to wither as Tim's obsession with financial control intensified. Anna longed for the days when their relationship was built on trust and compromise. Tim had to confront his need for control and rediscover the value of sharing financial decisions or risk losing the woman he loved.

How does financial control occur?

1.   **Fear and Insecurity:** One partner might feel a deep-seated fear of financial instability, perhaps due to past experiences or family history. This fear can drive them to exert control over their finances to ensure a sense of security. They may believe strict financial management is the only way to prevent financial disaster.

2.   **Differing Values:** Couples often enter marriage with different financial values and priorities. For instance, one may value saving for the future, while the other prefers spending on immediate gratification. The partner who likes saving may feel the need to control expenses to align them with their vision of responsible money management.

3.   **Lack of Trust:** Trust is the foundation of any healthy relationship. If trust has been eroded by previous financial mistakes or breaches of trust, one partner might assume control to prevent a recurrence. This can result in a lack of trust in the other's ability to make responsible financial decisions.

4.   **Gender Norms:** In some cases, traditional gender norms and societal expectations play a role. Historically, men have often been viewed as the primary breadwinners and financial decision-makers. This can lead to one partner assuming control based on societal expectations rather than on his or her actual financial expertise.

5.   **Perfectionism:** Some individuals have a strong desire for financial perfection. They want everything to be meticulously planned and executed according to their standards. This

perfectionism can lead to controlling tendencies as they believe that their way is the only correct way.

6.   **Communication Issues:** Poor communication in a relationship can exacerbate financial control. When couples struggle to discuss and compromise on financial matters, one partner may take control to avoid arguments and conflicts, believing it's the only way to maintain order.

7.   **Addiction or Compulsive Behaviour:** In some cases, financial control can be a result of addiction, such as gambling or overspending. One partner may control the other from accessing funds to fuel their habit.

Recognising that financial control can be detrimental to a relationship is essential. Open communication, compromise, and seeking financial advice or counselling when needed are effective ways to address these issues. In faith, we're encouraged to support one another and work towards unity in marriage, which includes healthy financial management based on trust, love, and shared values. Trusting in God's provision is a central theme in the Bible. In Matthew 6:25-34, Jesus teaches the importance of relying on God for our needs and not worrying about material possessions. This trust in God can alleviate the anxieties associated with financial control.

Effects of Financial Control on Marriage:
1.   **Power Imbalance:** One of the most noticeable effects is the power imbalance it creates. The controlling partner may make unilateral financial decisions, leaving the other feeling disempowered, disrespected and restricted in making financial decisions

2.   **Lack of Transparency:** Financial control can lead to a lack of transparency, with the controlling partner not fully disclosing financial matters. This can result in a lack of trust within the marriage.

3.   **Strain on Communication:** It can strain communication within the marriage. When one partner has sole control over finances, open discussions about money can become challenging, leading to misunderstandings and conflict.

4.   **Stress and Anxiety:** The lack of control can cause stress and anxiety. The non-controlling spouse might worry about their financial future, their ability to meet financial goals, and their family's well-being.

Income Disparities and Financial Equity

In the marriage journey, partners bring diverse backgrounds, experiences, and often, different income levels. These income disparities can create tension and conflict within a marriage. However, addressing these disparities and establishing financial equity within the partnership is not only crucial for the stability of the relationship but also aligns with biblical principles of fairness, unity, and love.

"Maria and Anton had once been the embodiment of love and happiness. Anton was a successful lawyer, earning a substantial income that afforded them a comfortable lifestyle. On the other hand, Maria was a dedicated preschool teacher who was passionate about her work. While she loved her job, it didn't come with the same financial rewards as Anton's legal career.

Resentment started to creep into their marriage. While proud of Anton's success, Maria couldn't help but feel envious of the financial freedom and status it brought. She longed for more time with him and the chance to enjoy some of the luxuries they could afford but seldom experienced. She began to wonder whether her teaching career was enough and if her contribution to their marriage was truly valued.

On the other hand, Anton felt the pressure to provide for the family, which strained his relationship with Sarah and the children. He became increasingly oblivious to their emotional needs, believing financial stability was the key to happiness. As Maria's resentment grew, she withdrew emotionally, and their once-joyful home became filled with tension and silent frustration.

The breaking point came when Anton purchased a luxurious vacation home without consulting Maria. He saw it as an investment for their future, but Maria perceived it as another instance of his disregard for her opinions and needs. The following argument was a tumultuous clash of emotions, hurtful words, and unmet expectations.

The destructive power of income disparities had torn through their once-loving marriage, leaving it in ruins. It became clear that financial success, while important, couldn't replace the fundamental need for emotional connection, respect, and understanding in a marriage.

This story serves as a poignant reminder of the potential destructive force of income disparities in a marriage. While money can provide comfort and security, it should never overshadow the significance of love, communication, and emotional connection within a partnership. Ultimately, it's not the size of the bank account that defines a marriage's success but the richness of the love and understanding shared between two people.

Addressing Income Disparities

1.   Accept one another: There is no place for feelings of inadequacy or superiority in a Christian marriage. "Be devoted to one another in love. Honour one another above yourselves." (Romans 12:10)

2.   Shared Financial Goals: Set shared financial goals as a couple. This includes short-term objectives like paying bills and long-term goals such as savings and investments. When both partners are invested in these goals, it helps create financial equity.

3.   Equal Sacrifice, Not Equal Contribution: In some cases, it may be unrealistic for both partners to contribute equally to

expenses or savings due to income disparities. Instead, aim for equal sacrifice. This means that both partners make proportional sacrifices to achieve financial goals. For example, if one partner earns significantly more, they might contribute more to shared expenses and savings.

4.   Budget Together: Create a budget as a couple that reflects both partners' financial realities. This budget should account for different income levels and prioritise shared goals. Regularly review and adjust the budget as needed.

Equitable Contribution to Expenses

1.   Proportional Contribution: In cases where income disparities are substantial, proportional contribution to expenses can be a fair approach. Each partner contributes a percentage of their income to shared expenses, ensuring that financial burdens are distributed fairly.

2.   Joint Accounts: Consider opening joint bank accounts for shared expenses, allowing both partners to contribute to bills and other financial obligations. This approach fosters transparency and unity in financial matters.

3.   Individual Accounts: While joint accounts can be beneficial, it's also essential to maintain individual accounts for personal expenses or discretionary spending. This arrangement respects each partner's autonomy while addressing shared expenses fairly.

Equitable Contribution to Savings

1.   Prioritise Savings: No matter the income level, it's important to prioritise savings and investments. The Bible encourages stewardship and planning for the future, as seen in Proverbs 21:20: "The wise store up choice food and olive oil, but fools gulp theirs down."

2.   Equal Sacrifice for Savings: As with expenses, the focus should be equal sacrifice for savings. Both partners should

contribute a portion of their income towards shared savings goals, even if the amounts differ.

3.   Emergency Fund: Building an emergency fund is critical for financial stability. Both partners can contribute according to their means to ensure this fund is well-funded.

Addressing income disparities and establishing financial equity in a marriage is a practical necessity and aligns with biblical principles of unity, fairness, and love. By focusing on open communication, shared financial goals, and equitable contributions to both expenses and savings, couples can navigate income disparities successfully.

Nurturing a Healthy Marriage - Overcoming Marital Discord

Another heated argument erupted between Phil and his wife, Janet. His voice thundering, Phil implored, "Do you ever read your Bible?" His fists pounded on the dining room table. "God has designated the husband, not the wife, to lead. I'm in charge, and you are supposed to submit and obey my every word! I'm the breadwinner here, and if I desire a new car, God grants me the authority. Keep your nose out of our finances."

Janet enthusiastically retorted, "Fine, go ahead and get your car! I'm certain it will impress your racing buddies. I'm out of here! My friends and I will enjoy a week at the resort and spa. Goodbye!"

One fact stands out: disputes over money are rarely just about finances. They often serve as manifestations of deeper marital issues. The most effective solution typically involves husbands and wives embracing their biblical roles.

Love and respect

The heartening news is that when a wife genuinely respects her husband in ways meaningful to him, it kindles within him a sense of love for his wife. Her most profound need - to feel loved - finds fulfilment. Similarly, when the husband loves his wife in ways that resonate with her, she responds respectfully, satisfying his greatest need.

There is no valid justification for a husband to assert, "I will love my wife once she respects me," or for a wife to claim, "I will respect my husband once he loves me."

Emerson Eggerich, the author, aptly notes, "When a husband feels disrespected, he naturally responds in ways that feel unloving to his wife. When a wife feels unloved, she instinctively reacts in ways that feel disrespectful to her husband. Without love, she reacts without respect. Without respect, he reacts without love." [5]

Healing and Reconciliation

The Bible offers guidance on reconciling different spending habits within a marriage, emphasising principles that promote unity, respect, and financial harmony.

1. Seek God in Prayer: Begin by seeking God's guidance through prayer. Ask for wisdom, patience, and a compassionate heart to address financial conflicts that align with biblical principles.

2. Communicate Truthfully: Ephesians 4:25 encourages honesty: "Therefore each of you must put off falsehood and speak truthfully to your neighbour, for we are all members of one body." Open and honest conversations about money are essential.

3. Discuss Priorities: Both partners should discuss their financial priorities, values, and goals openly. This dialogue can help create understanding and facilitate compromise.

4.   Acknowledge Your Differences: Recognize that you and your partner may have different money personalities, and that's okay. Rather than trying to change each other, embrace your individual strengths and weaknesses. Accept each other and create safe environments to speak the truth without fear (Phil 2:1-2). Realise God's unique design for the couple and each other's roles (Gen 2:24)

5.   Create a Budget: Develop a budget incorporating both partners' input. This budget should provide room for your unique spending habits and ensure that both of you have a say in financial decisions. Design tools to solve common problems (for example, discuss spending above a specific limit, a regular financial evaluation together, use joint accounts)

6.   Seeking Wisdom and Counsel: Proverbs 13:10 encourages seeking wisdom: "Where there is strife, there is pride, but wisdom is found in those who take advice." Seeking advice from financial counsellors, marriage mentors, or trusted individuals can provide valuable insights and help couples make informed decisions.

7.   Mutual Respect and Submission: Ephesians 5:21 calls for mutual submission: "Submit to one another out of reverence for Christ." In the context of finances, this means respecting each other's opinions and finding compromises that reflect the mutual submission demanded by the Bible. It's essential to acknowledge the value of each partner's perspective.

8.   Financial Accountability: Proverbs 27:23 advises, "Be sure you know the condition of your flocks; give careful attention to your herds." Financial accountability involves both partners staying informed about the family's financial situation. It can be achieved through regular budget meetings, shared financial goals, and transparency.

9.   Shared Financial Goals: Proverbs 24:27 (NIV) encourages planning: "Put your outdoor work in order and get your fields ready; after that, build your house." Couples can

align their spending habits by setting shared financial goals, prioritising savings, and creating a budget that reflects their values and objectives.

10. Colossians 3:13 (NIV) emphasises forgiveness: "Bear with each other and forgive one another if any of you has a grievance against someone. Forgive as the Lord forgave you." " In times of disagreement, a spirit of compromise and grace is essential. Both partners should be willing to meet in the middle and show understanding toward each other's spending habits.

Invest in financial education together. Attend financial workshops, read books, or seek advice from financial experts to enhance your financial literacy. Taking the Compass course, "Money and Marriage", can significantly help as you plan and develop your financial life together! Visit Compass' website at www.compass1.eu

Ultimately, a marriage that successfully reconciles after conflict reflects the biblical principles of unity, mutual respect, and love, ensuring that both partners can find financial harmony while growing together in their journey of love and faith.

Chapter 8: Planning your finances together

    Planning is a partnership, not only between marriage partners but also with God! As believers, we can plan in faith. If we align with God's wants, He will help us realise our plans. That is faith financial planning! We are told that "Whatever does not proceed from faith is sin." (Romans 14:23). So, what is faith? Again, the Bible tells us, "Now faith is the assurance of things hoped for, the conviction of things not seen." (Hebrews 11:1)

    Faith financial planning has everything to do with an eternal perspective, planning our finances to have the most lasting impact. This means spending time with the Lord and asking Him to put whatever He has in His heart in our hearts.

    "And without faith it is impossible to please him, for whoever would draw near to God must believe that he exists and that he rewards those who seek him" (Hebrews 11:6).

Set goals.

When the Lord gives us more than enough to live off, and we have been able to set aside some savings, it is important to set goals for using the surplus financial assets.

Goal setting always involves a tradeoff between the short-term and the long-term. If we don't have long-term goals, we won't know how to prioritise spending and saving in the short term.

Money is a tool to accomplish our goals and objectives, and setting goals clarifies how to allocate money towards our savings, investments, debt repayment, or sharing.

Having written goals makes it far more likely that we will be disciplined and maintain good financial habits. Habits take root in our lives when we have a strong 'why' motivating them.

Goals provide the 'why' and the necessary motivation. Knowing why we are doing something via a written goal helps us create a starting point, stay the course, and know when we are done and can look to new goals. Proverbs 29:18 says, "Where there is no revelation, people cast off restraint; but blessed is the one who heeds wisdom's instruction." Writing goals is a way to clarify the revelation God has given us for our lives. Pursuing them provides a pathway and helps us make more confident decisions today.

As followers of Christ, we are privileged to be able to set goals with God's input and vision. One of my favourite verses says, "For we are His creation, created in Christ Jesus for good works, which God prepared ahead of time so that we should walk in them" (Ephesians 2:10, HCSB).

God has already prepared works for us to do. When we ask Him to speak into our goals, He can move us into those works and allow us the privilege of completing them. Without goals, our financial decisions are dictated by other people, unchecked emotions, and perceived urgency – all of which obstruct wise decision-making. Most of us operate by accumulating as much as possible, which is the world's way of thinking. Since the longing for more is insatiable, we never experience financial peace and rest.

Only a Christian can set faith goals and ask, "God, what do you want me to achieve?" This is a way to experience the hand of God in my financial situation. A faith goal is a statement: "I believe that God is calling me to_____________ (fill in the blank).

I need to be wholeheartedly committed to internalising and acting on this statement. I believe that goals;
1. Give direction and purpose,
2. Help crystallise thinking and
3. Provide personal motivation.

To build confidence that God will direct my steps, it helps to visualise the following sequence.
1. My goal-setting comes from God.
2. I seek His will and His wisdom.
3. I start to move.
4. He directs my steps.

"To humans belong the plans of the heart, but from the LORD comes the proper answer of the tongue. All a person's ways seem pure to them, but motives are weighed by the LORD. Commit to the LORD whatever you do, and he will establish your plans" (Proverbs 16:1-3).

Setting long-term goals while you are young is vitally important. If you don't, years go by without appropriate intermediate steps, and you eventually end up dealing with long-term goals as though they were short-term because the short-term is all you have left. Long-term goals are much more difficult to finance on a short-term basis, but setting aside a small amount over a long period will help you build assets to meet them.

Planning my finances with God and my wife has been a rewarding exercise to help us realise our long-term goals.

Goals should be specific, measurable, achievable, and realistic, and we should know when they have been achieved.

Setting a finish line for our goals will give us an indication of when we can stop accumulating. I talked to an accountant who told me that quite a few wealthy individuals who he is advising have accumulated enough to reach their long-term goals many times over. When we have reached our predetermined finish line by building assets sufficient to meet these goals, the surplus can be directed to extra generosity.

Borrowing

Borrowing is not prohibited in the Bible, but it warns against the dangers. Should we find ourselves in a situation where we cannot meet the payments, the Bible says this is morally wrong. "The wicked borrow and do not repay, but the righteous give generously." (Psalm 37:21). When we borrow, we are presuming that in the future, we will be able to meet payments, but we do not know what the future will be like. (See James 4:13-15.) Borrowing may prevent God from an opportunity to provide for our needs, as He promised.

We should borrow only for projects that promote human flourishing. Examples could be home ownership, a college education, starting a business, or essentials for work. Consumer borrowing is always economically bad. Wait, save, and pay cash!

If borrowing is necessary, follow these three rules:

1. The economic return must be greater than the economic cost;
2. I must have a guaranteed way to repay;
3. Both partners must agree with one another.

Are you borrowing for a car or saving?

Couples have to decide whether to borrow or save when acquiring a car. From a Biblical perspective, this choice can be seen through the lenses of wisdom, stewardship, and financial responsibility. Borrowing for a car is a convenient option, allowing immediate access to a vehicle without the need for substantial savings. However, it's essential to evaluate this decision within the framework of biblical principles.

Borrowing entails a commitment to repay, often with interest, which can lead to financial bondage. "The borrower is slave to the lender." (Proverbs 22:7)

Furthermore, Romans 13:8 encourages believers to "owe no one anything, except to love each other." This verse highlights the importance of financial responsibility and avoiding unnecessary debts. Borrowing for a car may not align with this principle if it leads to burdensome repayments and financial stress.

On the other hand, saving for a car aligns more closely with biblical values. It reflects the principles of stewardship, discipline, and wise financial management. Proverbs 21:20 reminds us, "Precious treasure and oil are in a wise man's dwelling, but a foolish man devours it." Saving demonstrates wisdom in planning for future needs and managing resources responsibly.

Moreover, saving allows individuals to avoid the entanglements associated with borrowing. They can acquire a car without debt by patiently accumulating the necessary funds.

I have never bought a new car in my 50 years of driving! A new car never ever appreciates in value! Our ego could easily justify buying a new car, but it never makes economic sense. I have discovered that the cheapest car you will ever drive is the one you currently have. The cost of financing, depreciation, and the lost financial opportunities when buying a new car will always offset the maintenance of an older car. I am currently driving a 14-year-old car and plan to keep it for some time.

My wife and I had a great experience of waiting on the Lord for His timing and provision. I gave up my job as CEO of a chemical company to join a mission organisation dedicated to reaching businesspeople for Christ. I needed a car, but I had to return my company car. We didn't want to borrow to buy one but decided to trust that the Lord would provide. This meant waiting and praying. Eventually, we were given a Mercedes 300 and didn't have to touch our savings, which we would need to supplement our income.

Navigating a mortgage in uncertain times

Obtaining a mortgage to purchase a house is a significant financial decision, and it's essential to approach it with wisdom, prudence, and consideration of the potential challenges, particularly in a climate where house prices may fall, and interest rates could increase.

John and Sarah, a young couple, enthusiastically bought their new house, picturing a bright future for their growing family. The house seemed perfect. However, several years later, their dreams collided with the harsh realities of an unpredictable housing market.

High interest rates and a fluctuating economy made their mortgage payments increasingly burdensome. At the same time, house prices began to plummet, and the once-valuable investment became a financial burden.

The couple faced a dilemma as John received a promising job offer in a different city. Moving for the job would mean selling their house at a significant loss, leaving them with a substantial mortgage deficit. They found themselves trapped, unable to take the job opportunity that could improve their lives.

With heavy hearts, they had to decline the job offer and continue struggling to make ends meet. Their story serves as a poignant reminder of the challenges many face in navigating a housing market filled with uncertainties. Ultimately, they clung to hope, knowing that the tide might turn in their favour someday, and they could set sail toward a brighter future.

A mortgage should be manageable within your financial means, accounting for possible fluctuations in interest rates and property values.

James 4:13-15 encourages believers to consider the uncertainty of the future when making plans. In a mortgage, this means being prepared for economic fluctuations, possibly falling house prices and rising interest rates. Creating an emergency fund and evaluating various scenarios can help you navigate these uncertainties.

Taking a mortgage on a house, especially in a volatile market, should be approached with caution and wisdom. By evaluating your financial stability, avoiding excessive debt, preparing for uncertainty, seeking counsel, and prioritising contentment, you can make a mortgage decision that aligns with biblical principles and safeguards your financial well-being in the face of potential challenges.

My wife and I bought our first home in 1978. We have stayed there ever since. Now that the mortgage has been paid off, we can live off less income in our retirement years. We celebrated, thankfully, when the mortgage was paid off. What a sense of freedom! We encourage everyone to become free from mortgage debt as soon as possible.

Seven major areas in which to set goals.

Here is a description of seven major areas in which goals can be set.

1. Homeownership

Here are a few ways that investing in home ownership can benefit you:

- Homeownership can be a great way to build wealth and create a sense of stability and security.
- Appreciation: The value of a property can appreciate over time, which can result in a significant return on investment.
- Tax benefits: Mortgage interest may be tax-deductible (depending on national conditions), which can help reduce your overall tax bill
- Equity: As you make mortgage payments, you are building equity in your home, which can be used as collateral for loans or as a source of cash in the future.
- Stable housing costs: Renting a property can result in unpredictable housing costs, whereas a fixed-rate mortgage can provide more stability and predictability regarding housing expenses.
- Sense of community: Owning a home can provide a sense of community and belonging and can be an excellent way to establish roots in a neighbourhood.

However, it's important to remember that buying a home also comes with risks. The value of a property can also depreciate, and the housing market can be affected by factors such as interest rates and economic conditions. It's also important to consider whether you can afford the costs associated with home ownership, such as mortgage payments, property taxes, and maintenance costs.

2. Financial independence

Financial independence is when an individual has enough wealth to support their lifestyle without relying on regular employment or government benefits. Financial independence is often associated with retirement but can also refer to the ability to leave a job or take time off to pursue other interests.

As believers, we work from the principle of being financially dependent on the Lord as our Provider. There is also no such thing as retirement for the believer, as we are commanded to continue to work as a calling from God and an essential part of our life as disciples. However, we can live off the income from our investments and work without being dependent on paid employment!

Financial independence can be achieved through saving, investing, and building a diverse portfolio of assets.

Some key characteristics of financial independence include:

•	Passive income: Financial independence requires having a reliable source of passive income, such as rental properties, dividends, or interest.

•	Low living expenses: Financial independence is more accessible if you can keep your expenses low.

•	Investment in diversified assets: A diversified portfolio of assets, including stocks, bonds, and real estate, can provide a steady income stream.

•	Savings and budgeting: Financial independence requires having enough savings to support your lifestyle without relying on regular employment.

•	Minimal debt: Financial independence is more accessible if you have minimal debt and can avoid taking on new debt.

Reaching financial independence can take many years, and it is a journey that requires discipline, patience, and a long-term perspective.

3. Education

You can set a goal to save for the cost of education for your children and your grandchildren or to spend on someone from a developing nation. A college education can be expensive and can put a significant financial burden on families. The cost of tuition, room and board, books and supplies, and other expenses can add up quickly and may be difficult to afford without proper planning and saving. Here are some reasons why saving for college fees is important:

- Financial stability: Saving for college can help alleviate the financial burden of paying for college and allow families to plan for the cost in advance.
- Access to better opportunities: A college education can open up better job opportunities and lead to higher earning potential in the long run.
- Avoiding student debt: Saving for college can help reduce or avoid the need for student loans, which can have a long-term impact on an individual's financial stability.
- Tax benefits: Some college savings plans may offer tax advantages to help families save more for college.
- Preparing for the future: Saving for college can help prepare for the future and set children up for success in their education and careers.

It's never too early or too late to start saving for college. The earlier you start, the more time you have for your savings to grow. Saving for college can involve a combination of personal savings and financial aid. It's essential to start planning early and explore different savings options, such as savings accounts, college savings plans, and scholarships.

4. Retirement

Building a retirement fund is important because it provides a financial safety net for when an individual can no longer work and earn an income. Without a retirement fund, individuals may have to rely on Social Security or other government benefits, which may not be enough to maintain their standard of living. A retirement fund can also ensure that an individual has enough money to pay for healthcare expenses, which tend to increase as people age.

Here are some reasons why building a retirement fund is essential:

• Financial peace: A retirement fund can provide financial peace, knowing you have capital to fall back on when you retire. Your retirement age comes quicker than you realise!

• Maintaining standard of living: A retirement fund can help you maintain your standard of living after you retire and avoid having to make drastic changes to your lifestyle.

• Meeting healthcare expenses: As people age, healthcare expenses tend to increase; a retirement fund can help you meet these expenses.

• Avoiding dependence on government benefits: A retirement fund can help you avoid relying on government benefits such as Social Security, which may not be enough to maintain your standard of living.

• Tax benefits: Many retirement savings plans offer tax advantages that can help you save more for retirement.

It's essential to start building a retirement fund as early as possible so your money has more time to grow and compound. Building a retirement fund requires a consistent effort over time, and it's important to have a plan and stick to it.

5. Generosity

Saving for a large donation can be a great way to support a cause or organisation you are passionate about.

Setting a specific savings goal and creating a plan can help you stay motivated and on track to reach your target.

It's important to remember that saving for a large donation may take time and discipline. Still, significantly contributing to a cause you care about can be gratifying. It's also important to research the organisation and ensure that the donation aligns with your values and that the organisation uses the funds effectively.

6. Legacy

Leaving a financial legacy refers to passing on wealth and assets to future generations, which can be an important aspect of financial planning. Here are some reasons why leaving a financial legacy is important:

- Providing for future generations: A financial legacy can ensure that future generations have the resources to achieve their goals and dreams, such as buying a house, starting a business, or pursuing higher education.
- Maintaining family values and traditions: A financial legacy can help to preserve family values and traditions by providing the resources needed to support them.
- Passing on wisdom and knowledge: A financial legacy can also be an opportunity to pass on wisdom and knowledge about money management, investing, and financial planning to future generations.
- Charitable giving: A financial legacy can also be used for charitable giving and philanthropy, positively impacting the community and society.
- Estate planning: A financial legacy also involves estate planning, which can help to ensure that assets are distributed according to an individual's wishes and to minimise taxes and other expenses.

It's important to remember that leaving a financial legacy is not just about passing on money and assets but also values, traditions, and life lessons. Building a financial legacy often requires careful planning and a long-term perspective. Working with a financial advisor and legal professional is critical to ensure your assets are protected and distributed according to your wishes.

7. Business

Investing in someone's business can help them start and grow their company. It can be a great way to provide financial support, mentorship, and guidance.

There are several ways to invest in a business, including:

• Equity investment: This involves buying company shares, which gives the investor ownership and a percentage of the profits.

• Debt investment: This involves lending money to the business and receiving interest and principal payments in return.

• Angel investment: This type of equity investment is where an individual investor, an 'angel,' provides capital to a start-up in exchange for ownership equity.

• Crowd investing: This is a method of raising money by appealing to many people, typically via the internet. Crowd-investing platforms allow individuals to invest small amounts of money in a business in exchange for rewards or equity.

Investing in a business can be a great way to help someone start and grow their own company, but it's essential to remember that it also comes with risks. It's important to conduct thorough research and due diligence to understand the business model, the industry, and the management team before investing. It's also essential to set clear expectations and agreements with the business owner to ensure the investment aligns with your goals and investment strategy.

Chapter 9: Pursuing Financial Freedom

Financial freedom is a profoundly transformative journey in which a couple experiences liberation from financial anxiety, worry, materialism, and debt. It's not merely about accumulating wealth; it's about embracing a purposeful life, free from the shackles of financial stress and centred on the things that truly matter. In the context of a marriage, the pursuit of financial freedom becomes even more significant as it fosters a strong, harmonious, and thriving partnership. Let's delve into the importance of financial freedom for couples and its profound impact on their lives.

God wants us to remain free. "For freedom Christ has set us free; stand firm therefore, and do not submit again to a yoke of slavery" (Galatians 5:1, ESV). The source of our freedom is knowing the truth about what God has to say about money in the Bible. Jesus said, ". . . If you abide in my word, you are truly my disciples, and you will know the truth, and the truth will set you free" (John 8:31-32, ESV).

Financial freedom is indeed independent of the actual amount of money one possesses. It's a concept rooted in how a couple manages their financial resources rather than the size of those resources. Here's why financial freedom transcends the mere accumulation of wealth:

- **Mindset and Behavior**: Financial freedom is primarily about one's mindset and behaviour concerning money. It involves making wise financial choices, living within one's means, and avoiding unnecessary debt. It's not limited to those with high incomes; individuals with modest incomes can achieve financial freedom by practising sound financial habits.

- **Living Within Your Means**: Financial freedom doesn't depend on how much you earn; it's about living within your means. This means spending less than you earn and making responsible financial choices. People who earn a lot but spend even more may not experience financial freedom, while those with more modest incomes who manage their money wisely can achieve it.

- **Debt Management**: Managing debt is crucial to financial freedom regardless of income. Those burdened by high levels of debt, regardless of income, may not experience financial freedom. On the other hand, someone with a lower income who avoids accumulating debt can achieve financial freedom more easily.

- **Emergency Funds**: Having an emergency fund is a significant aspect of financial freedom. It ensures you're prepared for unexpected expenses and can avoid going into debt to cover them. The size of your emergency fund is determined by your financial situation, not your income level.

- **Satisfaction and Contentment**: Achieving financial freedom often involves finding contentment with what you have rather than constantly striving for more. Contentment and satisfaction can be attained at any income level, leading to a sense of financial freedom.

Financial freedom is a state of financial well-being that transcends the size of your income or the amount of money you possess. It's about adopting sound financial practices, living within your means, and making informed decisions about your money. You can pursue financial freedom by developing the right financial mindset and behaviours regardless of your income level.

. It fosters a harmonious partnership, strengthens the emotional connection, and allows them to embrace a life rich in purpose and shared experiences. As couples navigate the path to financial freedom together, they discover that it's not just about the destination but also the profound positive impact it has on their journey and the quality of their lives.

Contentment

Learning to be content is crucial in pursuing financial freedom. Contentment is not the fulfilment of our desires but the appreciation of what God gives us and the freedom to share it! The fruit of contentment is a wonderful state of being in which body, soul and spirit are in harmony and at peace.

Contentment is not striving for more and more, not fulfilling all our desires, but finding joy in whatever circumstances you find yourself in. It is neither complacent nor inactivity - it is a positive discipline where we learn to enjoy 'enough.' Contentment looks up - not around!

Consider what the apostle Paul said about contentment. "I am not saying this because I am in need, for I have learned to be content whatever the circumstances. I know what it is to be in need, and I know what it is to have plenty. I have learned the secret of being content in any and every situation, whether well fed or hungry, whether living in plenty or in want. I can do everything through him who gives me strength." (Philippians 4:11-13)

Contentment must be learned. It is not something that comes easily.

It is not dependent on any amount of money but on the source of our provision.

Contentment is finding a balance in our spending. Consider the prayer of Agur in Proverbs 30:8. "Two things I ask of you, O LORD; do not refuse me before I die: Keep falsehood and lies far from me; give me neither poverty nor riches, but give me only my daily bread. Otherwise, I may have too much and disown you and say, 'Who is the LORD?' Or I may become poor and steal and so dishonour the name of my God."

He is not asking for any amount of money, merely 'daily bread.' – only what is needed for daily living. He goes on to say that if he should have too much, he could start trusting in money and neglect God. If he should have too little, he could take things into his own hands and get what he needs in a dishonest way.

Either way – God would be dishonoured.

How much is enough?

This is a straightforward question to ask but difficult to answer, but the answer, when found, will lead to financial freedom, being able to say 'no' to more and being thankful for what we have.

The Greek philosopher Epicurus stated, "Nothing is enough for the man to whom enough is too little." Contrast that with the well-known answer to our question from J.D. Rockefeller, which, although stated over a hundred years ago, has characterised our capitalist system recently. When asked 'how much is enough', he said 'just a little bit more!'

Prof. Dr. Thomas Sedlacek tackled the problem of being unable to answer our question. In his book, "The Economics of Good and Evil." [6]

"The more we have, the more we want. Why? Perhaps we thought (and this sounds truly intuitive) that the more we have, the less we will need. We thought that consumption leads to saturation of our needs. But the opposite has proven to be true. The more we have, the more additional things we need. Every new satisfied want will beget a new one and leave us wanting. For consumption is like a drug."

If the question of enough is not answered, we will always be left wanting, according to Sedlacek, becoming victims to 'affluenza', the sickness of our times, for which the cure is the answer to our question.

Anselm Grün is a Franciscan monk and director of a large group of enterprises employing over 600 people in southern Germany. He leads these enterprises according to Franciscan rules. In his 2015 book "Gier" (Greed), [7] he agrees with Sedlacek, arguing that the attitude of never having enough leads to very unrestful behaviour, a nomadic existence and continual dissatisfaction. *"When we desire possessions, we are looking for rest which we never find because we ultimately discover that the possessions possess us and lead us into more needs."*

The desire for possessions is a desire for rest. But the paradox is that we never find rest because the desire for more possesses us. Grün says furthermore that if we do not set a limit and declare 'enough'! Then, we will develop what he calls a nomadic behaviour – always looking for the next big thing – the next thrill. We are never satisfied and, therefore, not at rest with ourselves.

He says we will never be at rest and become possessed by the desire for more … Jesus came to set us free … not to become 'possessed' by anything apart from Him.

E.F. Schumacher captured This thought succinctly in his seminal book "Small is Beautiful." [8]

He states, "The cultivation and expansion of needs is the antithesis of wisdom. It is also the antithesis of freedom and peace. Every increase of needs tends to increase one's dependence on outside forces over which one cannot have control and therefore increases existential fear. Only by a reduction of needs can one promote a genuine reduction in those tensions which are the ultimate causes of strife and war."

He agrees with Grün and says that expanding needs is the exact opposite of peace and freedom. If we do not limit spending, we will become dependent on outside forces, such as advertising, pressure from friends & our culture of consumerism.

Listening to Sedlacek, Grün and Schumacher, we can conclude that the answer lies in limiting our needs and desires and developing a sober lifestyle of sufficiency in which we can be content and thankful for all God has given us to enjoy. If we do not pursue such a path, we become subject to inward desires and outside forces which control us, resulting in loss of freedom.

Enough for what?

The short answer is; enough for everything God wants you to do. An old friend said, "Remember, God always pays for what He orders!   His promise remains true. "And God is able to make all grace abound to you, so that having all sufficiency in all things at all times, you may abound in every good work." (2 Corinthians 9:8)

He will provide enough to abound in every good work - whatever He prepares for us to undertake. Do I believe God can provide all I need for all He asks me to do?

Trusting in His provision leads to financial freedom. It all stems from His grace, His unmerited favour - out of His resources, not ours! We need to start thanking Him that He is providing 'sufficient' = enough!

Freedom from debt

Marriage is a sacred bond, a partnership, and a journey that encompasses all aspects of life, including finances. When overdebt rears its ugly head in a marriage, it can become a significant source of stress and strain on the relationship. However, the Bible offers valuable guidance on managing debt and achieving financial freedom. In this blog article, we will explore overdebt in marriage from a biblical perspective and provide insight on the path to financial liberation.

"David and Jacqueline had been living the dream: a beautiful home, luxury cars, and indulgent vacations. They couldn't resist the allure of an extravagant lifestyle, living in the moment and borrowing against their future.

Overdebt crept in silently like a shadow growing longer as the sun set. Their credit cards bore the weight of their desires, and the mounting bills multiplied. Dining at fine restaurants, weekend shopping sprees, and exotic getaways had become their way of life. The consequences began to surface.

One evening, as they confronted their mountain of debt, David and Jacqueline sought guidance from their faith and biblical principles. They realised their materialistic desires overshadowed their commitment to financial stewardship, contentment, and unity.

They began by humbling themselves and praying for strength and wisdom. They opened a dialogue, addressing the debt head-on, and planned to tackle it together. They decided to trim their expenses, focus on essential needs, and commit to a debt repayment plan.

Their faith sustained them throughout the journey. As they paid off their debts systematically, David and Jacqueline experienced financial freedom and the renewal of their marriage. The struggle had brought them closer, and they discovered that true wealth lay not in possessions but in love, unity, and the peace that comes with responsible stewardship. Overdebt had been a harsh teacher, but it had also shown them the path to financial redemption and a more profound understanding of what truly matters in life.

Consequences of Overdebt:

• Stress and Tension: The weight of debt casts a dark cloud over marriage. What was once a loving relationship now feels strained and distant.

• Sleepless Nights: Countless sleepless nights are often spent worrying about the financial predicament. Money becomes a relentless source of anxiety.

• Lack of Financial Security: The dream home and the expensive cars feel more like burdens, and the fear of losing everything looms.

• Marital Strain: Frequent arguments erupt over how to tackle the debt. Trust is eroded, replaced by blame and resentment.

• Impact on Dreams: Aspirations like sending their children to the best schools or retiring early seem further out of reach.

Understanding Overdebt

Overdebt, or the burden of excessive debt, can infiltrate a marriage for various reasons, such as medical bills, student loans, credit card debt, or mortgages. It can lead to financial insecurity, stress, and conflict between partners.

The Bible says, "The rich rule over the poor, and the borrower is a slave to the lender" (Proverbs 22:7). Debt removes our freedom because our creditors gain the priority call on our finances; they must be paid first. If we don't pay them first, they take steps to enforce their priority.

Paul said, "All things are lawful for me, but not all things are helpful. All things are lawful for me, but I will not be dominated by anything." (1 Corinthians 6:12). Borrowing is not forbidden in the Bible, but it's always discouraged because we become dominated by it, and it removes our freedom.

If we do not pay our debts back on time, tension builds. The one to whom we owe money begins to wonder what kind of person we are. That relationship comes under stress and strain, and the first thing to go out the window is love; it gets replaced by a hostile creditor-versus-debtor relationship. It is tough to love our neighbour if we owe money that we cannot repay in full and on time; the relationship starts to break down.

Being anxious about paying back our loans and credit can lead to denial, fear, isolation, ill health, despair, and relationship breakdown.

Freedom from this kind of anxiety results in reduced stress and related illnesses, fewer family breakups, and even saved lives because stress can be a killer. This freedom enables people to give generously, order their finances based on their chosen priorities, and work on life goals.

Debt also removes our flexibility to adapt to unexpected circumstances.

Debt reduces our options, sometimes leaving only the most unpleasant. And it makes us less able to respond to God's call to do something different, including serving those in need.

Before deciding on a significant decision to borrow, we must pray and seek God's wisdom. "Search me, O God, and know my heart! Try me and know my thoughts! And see if there be any grievous way in me, and lead me in the way everlasting! (Psalm 139:23-24, ESV).

How to get out of debt

This is the most important goal to set. Achieving this goal will give you peace of mind. It is also the investment which will provide you with the highest return.

Here in The Netherlands., we pioneered a nationwide programme to help people out of debt. At the time of writing, the organisation we set up was able to help more than 10'000 people a year! We trained volunteers from churches to reach out into the neighbourhood and guide people to become debt-free.

A story from the Bible (2 Kings 4:1-7) was pivotal in our inspiration for this programme.

"The wife of a man from the company of the prophets cried out to Elisha, "Your servant my husband is dead, and you know that he revered the LORD. But now his creditor is coming to take my two boys as his slaves."

Elisha replied to her, "How can I help you? Tell me, what do you have in your house?" "Your servant has nothing there at all," she said, "except a little oil." Elisha said, "Go around and ask all your neighbours for empty jars. Don't ask for just a few. Then go inside and shut the door behind you and your sons. Pour oil into all the jars, and as each is filled, put it to one side."

She left him and afterwards shut the door behind her and her sons. They brought the jars to her, and she kept pouring. When all the jars were full, she told her son, "Bring me another one." But he replied, "There is not a jar left." Then, the oil stopped flowing.

She went and told the man of God, and he said, "Go, sell the oil and pay your debts. You and your sons can live on what is left."

The woman, whose husband had died and left her with debts she could not repay, was in dire straits. Tradition tells that her husband was Obadja, a court attendant to the wicked royal couple Achab & his wife Jezebel. He borrowed sums of money from Jehoram, son of Achab, the archenemy of the prophets, to buy food for the 100 prophets hiding in caves, fearing for their lives.

I realise it is easy from our vantage point, but I had to wonder - was it God's will to borrow money to meet their daily needs? I don't think so. This debt was not incurred by living beyond their means, although there was a severe drought at that time. It was, however, an attempt to do what only God can do - provide what we need to live.

She experienced the teaching of the proverb that debt robs you of your freedom: "Just as the rich rule over the poor, so the debtor becomes servant to the lender." (Proverbs 22:7)

The story about the widow suggests some steps to take to become free from the burden of debt.

1.   Go to the Lord first of all in prayer. She cried out to Elisha for help. Elisha immediately gave her hope by asking, "What can I do for you?" She then had to describe her predicament and bare her heart before God. When in debt, pray and ask the Lord to help. He can work in surprising ways!

2.   What do you have in the house? The next step is to see what you already have, which you can place into God's hands to work with. God always works with what we have and not with what we don't have.!

3.   She answered, "Nothing!" In fact, she had quite a lot going for her. She had a jar of oil, neighbours, her sons, the ability to work, selling skills - and God Himself! The Lord multiplied that which she placed in His hands.

4.   Elisha told her to 'close the door.' Close the door to the world and its distractions. Please don't listen to all the world telling us that we need to commit to no more debt.

5. She had to work first by producing and packaging the oil and then going to market and selling the oil. When in debt, we could produce more income by taking another job or a better-paid job. We could even look to sell some possessions to pay back debts.

6. Lastly, she had to repay her debts and 'live on what's left.' She and her sons were to live from what the Lord provided. This meant she had to live off a budget of the Lord's provision!

Navigating the 5 Stages of Debt as a Married Couple

Debt can be a typical financial challenge for married couples, and understanding the various debt stages can help navigate this journey. Recognising that debt can affect your financial well-being and your relationship is critical. Let's explore the five debt stages for a married couple and strategies to overcome them together.

Stage 1: Accumulation

Debt often starts with accumulating small balances from credit cards, loans, or unexpected expenses. At this stage, it's essential to communicate openly as a couple about your financial situation. Discuss your spending habits and create a budget to avoid further debt accumulation. Consider consolidating debts for more manageable payments.

Stage 2: Denial

In the denial stage, couples might downplay the severity of their debt or avoid addressing it altogether. It's crucial to acknowledge the reality of your financial situation. Have an honest conversation about the debt, and consult a financial advisor or counsellor if necessary. Facing the issue together is the first step toward a solution.

Stage 3: Conflict

Debt can strain a marriage, leading to conflicts about money and spending habits. To mitigate these disputes, work on your communication skills. Schedule regular financial meetings to discuss your goals, budget, and progress in debt reduction. Be open to compromise and find common ground in your financial decisions.

Stage 4: Action

In the action stage, couples take proactive steps to tackle their debt. Start by prioritising high-interest debts and creating a repayment plan. Explore strategies like the debt snowball method. Continue to maintain open communication and support each other throughout the process.

Stage 5: Freedom

Reaching the freedom stage is the ultimate goal. As a couple, you've successfully managed and reduced your debt. Celebrate your achievements and set new financial goals for the future. Consider redirecting the money you used to repay debt towards savings, investments, or experiences that enhance your relationship.

It's essential to work together, communicate openly, and develop a solid financial plan to navigate these stages successfully. Addressing debt as a team can improve your financial situation and strengthen your relationship. Remember that economic challenges are a common part of life; with determination and support, you can overcome them together.

Compass offers an online course to help you work through the stages of getting out of debt. Visit www.financialdiscipleship.academy

Chapter 10: The circle of financial freedom

Crafting a spending plan akin to a circle with three pivotal segments—obligations, needs, and desires—serves as a beacon guiding one's financial journey towards stability and mindful expenditure.

Your obligations are fixed costs, generally the same each month and easy to plan. These include mortgage or rent, water and energy, insurance and subscriptions. They represent responsibilities which demand timely attention and payments.

Your needs are variable expenses such as food, small items of clothing, personal care and entertainment.

Your desires are discretionary, larger purchases which you need to save for, like furniture, house maintenance, car expenses, and vacations.

The circle's visual representation underscores the significance of balance and prioritisation in financial planning. It urges individuals to honour obligations, address needs, and judiciously evaluate wants, fostering a disciplined approach to spending. It also illustrates that spending in one area influences what will be available to spend in another. There are no independent financial decisions.

Individuals gain clarity by delineating expenditure into these categories within the circle, allowing for informed decision-making. This holistic view enables the alignment of spending with financial goals, empowering individuals to achieve stability while fostering a healthier relationship with money.

The circle is simply a way of portioning your income according to three main categories – your obligations, needs and wants.

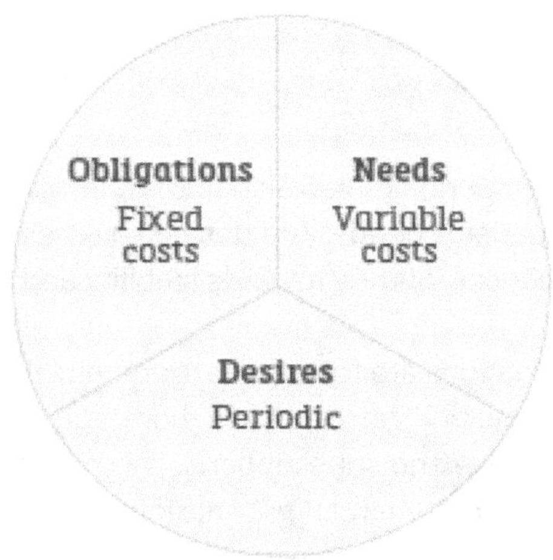

Everyone will have a different circle according to circumstances, responsibilities, and plans.

Each slice of the pie, or circle, is not necessarily the same size as depicted here. This illustration is only meant to show the idea of a circle of the main categories to spend or invest your income.

A Circle of Promise

The circle is first of all, a Circle of Promise. Jesus promises that if we

" Seek first the kingdom of God and his righteousness, and all these things will be added to you." (Matthew 6:33). So, what are 'all these things? They are everything we need to enjoy the life God has given us. They are everything we need to fulfil the role (s) that God has called us to perform in life.

A Circle of Peace

The circle is also a Circle of Peace. When we live in the circle of peace, we are free from worry, anxiety and fear of the uncertain future. The Biblical peace is 'shalom', which means 'wholeness, completeness.' Living in the circle of peace, or 'shalom', means living a balanced life in which our spending reflects the inner priorities of our hearts. Living in this circle of peace will free us from loving money, enabling us to be content with whatever we have. "Keep your life free from the love of money, and be content with what you have, for He has said, "I will never leave you nor forsake you." (Hebrews 13:5)

A Circle of Provision

The Circle of Provision enjoys and is thankful for all that God provides. Our Lord God is called "Jehovah Jireh" or 'the God who provides.' Paul could confidently tell the Christians in Philippi, "My God will supply every need of yours according to his riches in glory in Christ Jesus." (Philippians 4:19)

A Circle of Protection

When we live in the circle of protection, we can be assured of God's protection. "I have been young, and now am old, yet I have not seen the righteous forsaken or his children begging for bread"

(Psalm 37:25). God promises that if we honour Him by giving the tithe, the first tenth of our income, He will protect the rest. "I will rebuke the devourer for you, so that it will not destroy the fruits of your soil, and your vine in the field shall not fail to bear, says the Lord of hosts." (Malachi 3:11)

A Circle of Plenty

Lastly, we are developing a Circle of Plenty, of abundance. God does not merely want to provide whatever we need, but He desires to give us more than enough so that we can bless others. "And God is able to make all grace abound to you, so that having all sufficiency in all things at all times, you may abound in every good work." (2 Corinthians 9:7)

The importance of making a spending plan

Forming the circle is a way of developing a spending plan or a budget - an essential tool to plan your financial life together with God! For Christians, a spending plan is a spiritual tool which reminds us whose money we are managing.

We are using the words 'spending plan' and 'budget' together, meaning the same thing.! The word 'budget' turned up in English in the fifteenth century, having travelled via the French *'bougette'*, a diminutive form of *'bouge'*, meaning a leather bag. Its first meaning in English was "pouch, wallet, bag". Many associate 'budget' with restricting, hard work and discipline. However, the fruits of making a budget and sticking to it will provide great rewards.

A spending plan accurately shows our finances: we know how much is coming in and going out. This may seem obvious, but millions spend more than they earn monthly.

It helps us make informed choices about our spending: we can make different trade-offs in our choices, which are more challenging to make in the heat of the moment.

A spending plan establishes priorities by making us focus on our priority payments, those items which carry a penalty for non-payment (e.g. income tax, debt) and those items which really do matter to us, such as saving for our car (repairs), a wedding anniversary or a holiday.

It makes money go further because good planning resists casual spending and anticipates problems while there is time to address them or make adjustments.

A spending plan helps us reach our life goals, puts us back in control of our finances and helps us on the road to finding "financial freedom".

The Bible says we need to watch our financial interests closely. In Proverbs 27:23, we are advised to "know the state of your flocks ..." Today, we might say, 'Know the state of your stocks'. In other words, we need to know where our money is going.

Not knowing where your money is going equals disaster. You get into debt because you're not keeping good records showing what is happening with your finances. As Will Smith once said, 'You end up spending money you don't have on things you don't need to impress people you don't even like.'

And this causes all kinds of problems in your life. When you wonder where it all went, that is a warning sign. You are already in trouble if you don't know where your money is going because ignorance and easy credit equals trouble. You need to know what you owe, own, and earn. If you want your next ten years to be a decade of destiny, you must keep good records because riches can disappear quickly.

Think about this: if you spent as much time writing down your finances as you do worrying about them, you'd probably have much less to worry about. You must keep good records if you want God's blessing on your finances.

In Luke 14:28-29 Jesus says,

"For which of you, desiring to build a tower, does not first sit down and count the cost, whether he has enough to complete it? Otherwise, when he has laid a foundation and is not able to finish, all who see it begin to mock him, saying, `This man began to build, and was not able to finish."

Now, Jesus was not talking directly about our household budgets but about counting the cost of discipleship. How we manage money is an integral part of life and a big part of what it means to follow Jesus. Interestingly, Jesus talks about the risk of being mocked for failing to budget correctly because that is precisely what most of us do.

Five reasons why making a spending plan makes sense.
First of all, a spending plan will reduce conflict in marriage. Budgeting reduces conflict by providing built-in accountability and an objective standard for spending decisions. A couple can easily make 1500 to 2000 transactions each year. If you don't have a budget - a spending plan which allocates your income to reflect your priorities, any of these expenditures could touch after an argument.

Secondly, a spending plan allows you to create and maintain a vision for the future. A budget gives you the guidelines to successfully spend less than you earn, which is the key to long-term financial security.

If you want to buy a home, start your own business, fund your children's education, or plan for retirement, a spending plan can keep you focused on your goals.

Third, a spending plan brings unity into a marriage. It enables you to make objective and impartial decisions based on standard criteria. When our budget is drafted with input from both spouses, the spending for saving decisions is not mine or yours, but ours.

Fourth, a budget helps couples to communicate. You cannot establish a budget without discussing priorities, needs, goals, and dreams. Making a budget enables you to discuss priorities, how you make decisions, and how each unique personality contributes differently.

Lastly, establishing a budget sets an excellent example for your children. When your children see your financial discipline and how you are progressing towards reaching your goals, they will learn a valuable lesson on handling their money.

Designing your circle is a partnership with God.

In managing our finances, God has a part to play, and I have a part to play. Both have unique rights and responsibilities. I can never do what only God can, and He will not do what I must do.

God's part is to give us assignments, using money to enable us to carry out His wishes. "Calling ten of his servants, he gave them ten minas, and said to them, 'Engage in business until I come.' (Luke 19:13). God always pays for what He orders!

Part of God's unique role is providing for our needs and those around us! The same Lord, who provided manna in the desert, cared also for Elijah in his time of need. "You shall drink from the brook, and I have commanded the ravens to feed you there. And the ravens brought him bread and meat in the morning, and bread and meat in the evening, and he drank from the brook." (1 Kings 17:4,6)

A third aspect of God's role in finances is to use money to test us to see if He can trust us with greater responsibilities. "If you are faithful in little things, you will be faithful in large ones. But if you are dishonest in little things, you won't be honest with greater responsibilities." (Luke 16:10)

My part is using what He has entrusted to me faithfully, according to His wishes. "And if you are untrustworthy about worldly wealth, who will trust you with the true riches of heaven? (Luke 16:11).

To carry out His wishes, we must find out what they are through prayer and following the instructions given to us in the Bible, which equips us to manage our finances faithfully. "All Scripture is God-breathed and is useful for teaching, rebuking, correcting and training in righteousness, so that the man of God may be thoroughly equipped for every good work." (2 Timothy 3:16)

Live from the harvest of God's provision.
Our first responsibility is to recognise that the Lord will provide all we need for all He asks us to do. When Abraham was tested to see if he would obey God by sacrificing his most precious son, the Lord rewarded his willingness by providing a ram to be sacrificed. Abraham attributed the name Jehovah Jireh to God, which means *"The Lord will provide."*
We read in Genesis 22:14, "So Abraham called the name of that place, "The LORD will provide"; as it is said to this day, "On the mount of the LORD it shall be provided."
His provision is the harvest we can gather, our gross income.

"And God is able to make all grace abound to you, so that having all sufficiency in all things at all times, you may abound in every good work. As it is written, "He has distributed freely, he has given to the poor; his righteousness endures forever. He who supplies seed to the sower and bread for food will supply and multiply your seed for sowing and increase the harvest of your righteousness" (2 Corinthians 9:8-10).

The harvest consists not only of bread for food, which represents all we need for daily living but also seed to sow, representing money to invest in good works and generosity.

Closing your circle

Here, we introduce the concept of 'Closing Your Circle.' This means to limit your expenditure by making a plan, in prayer, together with God and, if appropriate, your partner. In 'Closing Your Circle', you say, "Lord, if you will provide what we have agreed, then that is enough for me to do all you ask. Thank you for what you provide, and I will be content with that. If you give me more, I will not spend it all on myself but use the excess I receive to bless my family and extend your Kingdom.

On the basis that God owns it all... I have to ask tough questions. "Lord, what do you want me to do with your money?" "Lord, how much of your money should I spend on myself?"

Once I have made my spending plan and my income has been apportioned into the various categories according to my priorities, closing the circle means stopping spending in all those categories.

Financial success is so simple. Spend less than you earn over a long period and be financially successful! It sounds simple, but it is not so easy to practise. When my circle is closed, I can ask the Lord for overflow!

An Open Circle
We will be tempted to expand our lifestyle and spend more on living! Outside pressure, such as advertising and peer pressure and inside pressure, such as greed or emotional

insecurity, will tempt us to spend more on our lifestyle. With a fixed income stream, giving will be the first area of our spending plan to be reduced or stopped. Then, there will be automatically less for future growth. There will be pressure to borrow to finance the expanding lifestyle and even great temptation to cheat on our taxes to gain more money to spend.

We must say 'no' to these outside pressures with which the world constantly tempts us to increase our spending. If I give into the world's standards, I will not be able to fulfil God's purpose for my life, be generous and reach my life goals.

"Do not love the world or the things in the world. If anyone loves the world, the love of the Father is not in him. For all that is in the world—the desires of the flesh and the desires of the eyes and pride of life—is not from the Father but is from the world. And the world is passing away along with its desires, but whoever does the will of God abides forever." (1 John 2:15,16)

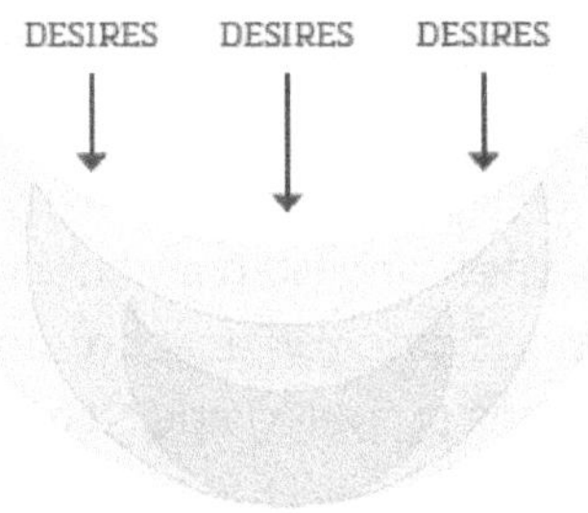

Living in an Open Circle means that you have not put a limit on your expenses. The circle expands when you are constantly focused on desires and buying more and more. A consequence is that whatever comes in - goes out. Spending increases due to the need to finance an ever-increasing lifestyle.

When spending exceeds income, several things are in danger of happening. You may have to borrow and go into debt, limiting your freedom. You may say, "I can't afford to give any more. I need the money."

Budget pressure could lead to dishonesty, cheating on expenses or taxes.

An overflowing circle

Overflow can be achieved in two ways. First of all, by earning more and secondly, by reducing my spending. Making

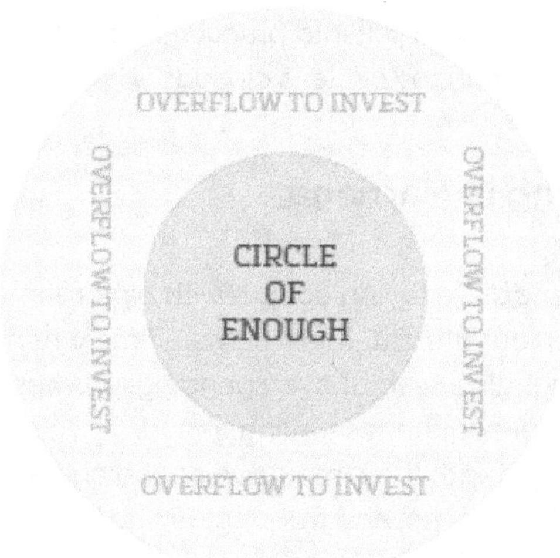

more is generally much more challenging to accomplish than spending less! If my circle is closed, any income I do not need for my circle flows over and can be utilised for my long-term goals.

Jesus stated clearly that the measure by which He can trust us with what He called " True riches" will be determined by how faithfu   l we are in using the money He has entrusted us with. True riches encompass 'treasures in heaven', an intimate relationship with Christ, and an abundant life. He also stated that giving would lead to abundance. "give, and it will be given to you. Good measure, pressed down, shaken together, running over, will be put into your lap. For with the measure you use it will be measured back to you." (Luke 6:38)

The Lord will not release this abundance if it is spent on an ever-increasing lifestyle. It will be released when we limit spending on ourselves and use the abundance to bless others.

Financial success is so simple. Spend less than you earn over a long period, and you will be financially successful! Sounds simple, but not so easy to put into practice! I can start asking the Lord for overflow when my circle is closed!

Overspending in Marriage

"David and Jill, a loving couple with big dreams, had always shared a harmonious life. But there came a time when they found themselves caught in a web of overspending, unaware of the symptoms and consequences lurking ahead.

It all started with their impulsive spending habits. The latest gadgets, designer clothes, and frequent dining out had become the norm. They often brushed off financial discussions, believing their love could conquer financial challenges.

Their credit card balances began to creep up, and they ignored the mounting debt, thinking they could pay it off later. The monthly bills arrived, and instead of addressing them together, David and Jill would hide them from one another, avoiding uncomfortable conversations about their finances.

As the overspending continued, the consequences became clearer. Stress and tension crept into their lives. They began arguing over money more frequently, turning once-loving conversations into bitter disputes. Their financial disarray had shaken the unity in their marriage, and they felt distant from one another.

The debt burden grew, and their ability to save for their future aspirations, such as buying a home or starting a family, became an unattainable dream. Financial insecurity loomed over them, casting a shadow on their once-bright future.

One evening, as they sat down to review their mounting bills and the credit card statements they'd hidden from each other, David and Jill finally realised the extent of their overspending problem. The stress and financial turmoil had become unbearable, and they knew they needed to take action.

They decided to seek guidance from a financial counsellor and to draw wisdom from their faith. Together, they reevaluated their financial goals and established a budget that allowed them to prioritise their dreams while curbing their impulsive spending.

As they embarked on their journey to financial recovery, David and Jill grew stronger as a couple. They learned valuable lessons about contentment, stewardship, and the importance of unity in financial decisions. Overcoming overspending wasn't easy, but they knew they could reclaim their financial stability with faith, communication, and discipline and rekindle the love and unity that had initially brought them together.

Money, often regarded as one of life's most significant stressors, can bring joy and turmoil to a marriage. Overspending, however, can strain the bonds of trust and unity. Thankfully, the Bible provides valuable insights on managing finances and achieving a harmonious financial life together.

Overspending in a marriage can stem from various root causes, such as differing money personalities, societal pressures, or unfulfilled emotional needs. Addressing these underlying issues is essential while drawing wisdom from the Bible.

Biblical Principles for Overcoming Overspending

1. Stewardship and Contentment: The Bible encourages us to be good stewards of the resources God has provided. Overspending can be seen as poor stewardship of finances.

Contentment is a virtue promoted in the Bible; we should be content with what we have rather than constantly seeking more. Philippians 4:11-12 says, "I have learned to be content whatever the circumstances."

2.   Avoiding Debt: The Bible advises against taking on excessive debt. Proverbs 22:7 states, "The rich rule over the poor, and the borrower is slave to the lender." Overspending and accumulating debt can lead to financial bondage, hindering one's ability to serve God and help others.

3.   Planning and Budgeting: Proverbs 21:5 teaches us that "the plans of the diligent lead to profit as surely as haste leads to poverty." Overspending often results from a lack of financial planning and budgeting. The Bible encourages careful planning to ensure responsible financial management.

4.   Prioritising Eternal Treasures: In Matthew 6:19-20, Jesus advises us to "store up for yourselves treasures in heaven." This reminds us to prioritise spiritual and eternal values over earthly possessions. Overspending on temporary pleasures can divert our focus from what truly matters.

5.   Avoiding Covetousness: The Tenth Commandment, "You shall not covet," found in Exodus 20:17, warns against desiring what others have. Overspending can be driven by a desire to keep up with others or acquire material possessions out of envy. The Bible encourages contentment and gratitude for what we have.

. By applying these principles, individuals can make better choices in handling their finances in line with their faith.

Steps to Overcome Overspending in Marriage

1.   Open Communication: Discuss your financial goals, concerns, and priorities openly. Encourage regular conversations about money and spending habits.

2. Set Common Goals: Establish shared financial goals, such as saving for a home, planning for retirement, or giving to charity. These shared objectives help you stay aligned.

3. Create a Budget: Develop a budget that includes both partners' input. A well-structured budget provides a framework for spending that can prevent overspending.

4. Accountability: Hold each other accountable for adhering to the budget and financial decisions. Regularly review your financial plan together.

5. Prioritise Giving: Embrace the biblical principle of generosity by allocating a portion of your income to charitable giving. This helps shift the focus from overspending on personal desires to supporting others in need.

6. Practice Self-Control: The Bible emphasises self-control as a fruit of the Spirit (Galatians 5:22-23). Cultivate self-discipline to resist impulsive spending.

7. Financial Education: Invest in financial education as a couple. Attend financial workshops or seminars together and read books on managing money wisely.

Overspending in a marriage can strain the relationship and hinder spiritual growth. However, couples can overcome overspending challenges by embracing biblical principles of contentment, stewardship, and unity. Remember that financial conflicts provide an opportunity for personal and spiritual growth. In seeking financial harmony, you strengthen your unity and deepen your connection with your partner and God.

Living off one income

Opting to live off one income while both partners work presents many advantages beyond financial stability. This intentional choice fosters a more holistic approach to life. Financial prudence and stability are notable advantages as they allow one income to be saved or invested, creating a safety net for unforeseen expenses or future aspirations like purchasing a home or planning for retirement.

Living off a single income can significantly reduce financial stress even with both partners employed. This arrangement cushions against economic uncertainties, allowing couples to navigate unexpected financial challenges without feeling strained.

The decision to live off one income provides flexibility in lifestyle choices. It enables pursuits such as further education, entrepreneurship, or dedicating time to personal passions without being solely dependent on both incomes.

Balancing work and life becomes more feasible when living off one income. With reduced financial pressure, couples can enjoy more leisure time, engage in family activities, or pursue personal interests, contributing to overall well-being.

Utilising one income for living expenses while saving or investing the other opens up opportunities for increased saving and investment potential. This strategy lays the groundwork for future financial growth and security.

This lifestyle choice often allows for a focus on family priorities. It may facilitate one partner staying home with children, reducing childcare costs and enabling a more hands-on approach to parenting.

Adopting this approach encourages shared financial goals, fostering unity in financial decision-making. It cultivates a collaborative mindset when managing and planning for the future. Even when both partners are working, living off one income is not just about financial savings but also about creating a more balanced, purposeful, and harmonious life that prioritises financial security, personal growth, and family well-being.

Compass offers an online course on making a spending plan. Visit www.financialdiscipleship.academy

Chapter 11: Raising children

As Jean and her husband observed their children joyfully playing, a hint of worry crept into Jean's expression. Reflecting on their upbringing, she confided in her husband, expressing a concern about the lack of financial education they received from their parents. Jean admitted that she and Allen might not be much better at imparting money management skills to their children. A pivotal question emerged: how could they instil a sense of responsibility and an understanding of the value of money in their kids? It was a moment of reflection and realisation for Jean, recognising the need for intentional financial guidance. As they navigate the challenges of parenthood, Jean and Allen are poised to explore strategies that blend practical lessons with a Biblical approach, ensuring their children grow up with a solid foundation in financial responsibility.

How prepared were you to make financial decisions when you left home? Parents and teachers spend 18 to 22 years preparing youth for occupations, but generally, less than a few hours teaching children the value and use of the money they will earn.

Here are some Biblical principles to help a couple prepare for the extra expenses associated with college-aged kids:

1.	**Stewardship and Financial Planning**: Practice responsible stewardship by creating a comprehensive financial plan. Plan for school and college expenses well in advance, budgeting for tuition, textbooks, and other costs. (Proverbs 21:5)

2.	**Saving and Wise Investments**: Establish a savings plan to accumulate funds for your children's education. Consider investments that align with your risk tolerance and long-term financial goals. (Proverbs 13:11)

3.	**Teach Financial Responsibility**: Instill financial responsibility in your children. Teach them the value of money, the importance of saving, and the consequences of debt. (Proverbs 22:6)

4.	**Seek Wise Counsel**: Consult with financial advisors or mentors who can provide guidance on college funding strategies. Seek advice from those with financial expertise (Proverbs 15:22).

5.	**Trust in God's Provision**: Trust in God's provision for your family's needs, including college expenses. Pray for guidance and trust that God will guide you through this financial journey (Matthew 6:33-34).

Teaching children about responsible financial management is essential. The Bible's teaching is clear, and we have found it to be so true. "Train up a child in the way he should go, even when he is old, he will not depart from it." (Proverbs 22:6)

Teaching and training children how to manage money is an invaluable life skill with far-reaching implications. By instilling financial literacy at a young age, we equip them with the tools to navigate the complex world of personal finance.

First and foremost, financial education fosters responsibility, teaching them to be good stewards. Children learn the value of earning, saving, and budgeting, developing a sense of accountability for their financial decisions. This early exposure helps them make informed choices as they grow, promoting financial independence.

Moreover, teaching kids about money encourages essential life skills such as critical thinking, patience, problem-solving, and self-discipline. It nurtures the ability to set goals, plan for the future, and make sound financial judgments. These skills extend beyond finances, benefiting their overall development.

Financial education also promotes resilience. Children learn that setbacks and financial challenges are part of life. They develop the skills to adapt and overcome obstacles, ultimately building their confidence and self-reliance.

Furthermore, instilling financial knowledge early can help break the cycle of debt and financial mismanagement. Children educated about money are less likely to fall into common financial pitfalls and develop a greater appreciation for financial security and stability.

Learning to handle money one step at a time is part of a child's education, a part that parents cannot leave to teachers but must direct themselves. Spending experiences are found in the outside world rather than in the classroom. Handling money – God's way is generally more caught than taught.

Fostering Financial Wisdom in Your Children

Here are some general tips to consider when raising financially savvy kids.

- **Lead by Example:** Demonstrate financial faithfulness to your children through your actions and decisions. Children absorb their parents' attitudes towards money like sponges, so setting a positive example is vital. In 1 Corinthians 11:1, Paul underscores the significance of being an example, saying, "Be imitators of me, just as I also am of Christ." As believers, we follow the ultimate model, Jesus Christ, who showed us how to live.

- **Effective Verbal Communication**: Verbally communicate God's principles of handling money to your children. Excellent studies, such as the Compass series, are designed for children of various age groups. Parents should explain why they manage money the way they do, emphasising the importance of their actions. Just as the Lord instructed the Israelites in Deuteronomy 6:6-7, we must diligently teach our children about God's ways. However, words alone are not enough; practical experiences are equally important.

- **Practical Experiences:** Create opportunities for your children to put into practice the financial principles they've learned. Each child has a unique personality and temperament, so tailor the training to their needs. These practical experiences should encompass money management (wise spending) and money-making (the value of work).

- **Income:** As soon as your children are ready for school, introduce them to an income they can manage. Parents must decide whether the children should earn this income through jobs or if it's provided as an allowance. The amount of income may vary based on factors like the child's age and ability to earn. What's most crucial is that children learn responsibility in handling money. Allow them to make mistakes and face the consequences; these experiences are valuable teachers.

- **Budgeting:** Teach your children how to budget as they receive an income. Begin with a simple system, using three jars labelled as "give," "save," and "spend." This visual method establishes a basic budget. As children grow, around the age of 12, they can start to learn about the family budget. They'll understand that they are growing up as they actively join in planning how the family's income will be spent. This involvement helps them recognise the financial limitations of the household and how to stretch money to meet the family's needs. Teaching children to be wise consumers, showing them how to distinguish between needs and wants, and instilling patience are important aspects of this training. Warn them about the influence of advertising and the danger of impulsive spending.

- **Giving:** Introduce the habit of giving to your children from a young age. Encourage them to donate gifts to a cause they can relate to and understand. This could be donating to a church project or providing food for a needy family they know. By involving children in giving, you demonstrate the value of meeting the needs of others and show them the impact of faithful generosity. Consider organising a family or church mission trip to a developing country when your children are teenagers. Direct exposure to poverty can profoundly impact and foster a lifelong commitment to helping those in need. Financial adoption of a child from a poor region is a good way to get them involved.

- **Understanding Debt**: Teach your children about the costs of borrowing money and the challenges of getting out of debt. Although we have never done this, I know of someone who loaned a teen some money for a bicycle and drew up a credit agreement with a repayment schedule that included interest. After he successfully paid off the loan, this achievement was celebrated with a "debt-burning" ceremony. Such a hands-on experience could help children appreciate the value of financial responsibility and avoid debt in the future.

Delayed Gratification

In my opinion, probably the most valuable skill a young person can learn is "delayed gratification."

Delayed gratification refers to the ability to resist the temptation of an immediate reward or pleasure in favour of obtaining a more substantial or valuable reward in the future. It involves exercising self-control, patience, and the capacity to temporarily tolerate waiting or enduring discomfort to achieve a greater, often more fulfilling outcome in the long run. This concept involves making choices that prioritise long-term goals or benefits over instant gratification or immediate desires.

The "Marshmallow Test" is a psychological experiment psychologist Walter Mischel conducted in the late 1960s and early 1970s. In this test, young children were offered a choice between an immediate reward (like a marshmallow) or the promise of a larger reward (two marshmallows) if they could resist eating the first marshmallow for a specific period, typically around 15 minutes.

The test aimed to measure a child's ability to delay gratification — the capacity to resist the temptation of an immediate reward in favour of a more substantial reward in the future. The results of this test were intriguing as they revealed a correlation between a child's ability to delay gratification and later life outcomes.

The extended studies following the children who participated in the Marshmallow Test showed compelling long-term effects. Those who demonstrated the ability to delay gratification tended to display several positive attributes in later life. They exhibited better academic performance, higher SAT scores, improved social and cognitive skills, better stress management, and overall greater success in various aspects of life.

Additionally, individuals who showed delayed gratification tendencies in childhood tended to have better long-term outcomes in areas such as health, financial stability, and relationships. The ability to resist immediate impulses and wait for a larger reward appeared to correlate with higher levels of self-discipline, resilience, and better decision-making skills later in life.

Financial challenges with children

Raising children is a rewarding journey, but it comes with financial challenges at each stage of a child's development. From the moment they arrive as infants to the time they transition into adulthood, parents must navigate a range of expenses, including childcare, education, extracurricular activities, and, in many cases, the daunting prospect of funding higher education. In this exploration of financial challenges when rearing children, we'll delve into the distinct financial hurdles parents face as their children grow and offer insights into managing these financial demands effectively, ensuring a stable and nurturing environment for the family.

Some general financial challenges include:

1. **Childcare Costs:** Childcare expenses can be one of parents' most substantial financial burdens. Whether it's daycare, a nanny, or after-school programs, the cost of quality childcare can strain a family's budget.
2. **Education Expenses:** Parents often need to plan for their children's education, including primary and secondary school costs, and save for college or vocational training. The increasing costs of education can be a significant financial concern.
3. **Healthcare Expenses:** Children require regular medical check-ups, vaccinations, and occasional medical care. Health insurance premiums, co-pays, and prescription costs can add up, impacting the family's budget.
4. **Housing Costs:** Families with children may need to consider a larger home, which often comes with increased

mortgage or rent payments, property taxes, and maintenance costs.

5. **Food and Clothing:** The more people in a household, the more significant the expenses for groceries and clothing. Growing children require new clothes and shoes regularly, and the grocery bill can increase with a growing family.

6. **Extracurricular Activities:** Children's extracurricular activities, such as sports, music lessons, or clubs, come with enrollment fees and equipment costs. Parents may also need to invest in transportation to and from these activities.

7. **Emergency Funds:** Having children often makes parents more aware of the need for an emergency fund. Unexpected medical bills or home repairs can arise anytime, and being financially prepared is essential.

8. **Life Insurance:** Parents often need life insurance to secure their family's financial future in case of a tragedy. The premiums for life insurance can be an ongoing expense.

9. **Estate Planning:** Couples with children must plan for their estate, including drafting wills and designating guardians. This may require legal fees and additional costs.

Teaching young children

Teaching children aged 6-12 about money is essential to building their financial literacy and instilling responsible money habits early in life. Implementing various age-appropriate strategies can effectively educate children about money management while making learning enjoyable and practical.

Compass offers books to teach children in age groups 6 to 8 and also from 8 to 12.

Here are some tips.

- **Introduce Basic Financial Concepts**: Begin with fundamental concepts like the value of money, different denominations, and the purpose of currency. Use real money or play money to illustrate these concepts, encouraging children to count and manage small amounts.
- **Allowance and Savings Jars**: Introduce the concept of earning money through chores or tasks. Provide a weekly or monthly allowance and encourage them to allocate portions to different jars or piggy banks for spending, saving, and sharing/donating. (See later) This teaches them budgeting and the importance of saving for goals.
- **Hands-On Learning Activities**: Engage children in practical activities like creating a pretend store at home where they can 'buy' and 'sell' using play money. Role-play situations such as making purchases, saving for toys, or setting up a lemonade stand help reinforce financial concepts in a fun way.
- **Grocery Shopping and Price Comparison**: Take children along for grocery shopping trips and involve them in comparing prices or finding discounts. Discuss the value of money, making choices based on needs versus wants, and staying within a budget.
- **Financial Games and Apps:** Utilise educational games or apps designed to teach kids about money. These tools often feature interactive activities, quizzes, or simulations that make learning about saving, spending, and budgeting enjoyable.
- **Help set Savings Goals**: Encourage children to set savings goals for items they wish to purchase. Whether it's a toy, a book, or a game, help them create a plan to save money gradually. Celebrate milestones as they get closer to reaching their goals.
- **Use Real-Life Scenarios**: Discuss real-life financial situations in a simplified manner. For example, talk about paying bills, budgeting for family activities, or the concept of loans by borrowing toys from friends and returning them.

- **Foster Open Communication:** Create an environment where children feel comfortable asking questions about money matters. Encourage curiosity and address their queries without judgment, fostering a positive attitude towards financial learning.

Teaching children aged 6-12 about money through interactive, age-appropriate activities cultivates a solid foundation in financial literacy. These strategies impart essential money management skills and instil positive attitudes towards earning, saving, and spending, setting the stage for responsible financial habits in the future.

Three Jars

The 'Three Jars' method is a simple yet effective technique used to teach children about money management, budgeting, and the importance of saving, spending, and sharing. It involves three separate jars or containers representing different financial categories:

Saving Jar: This jar is designated for saving money for future goals or larger purchases. Children allocate a portion of their allowance, or money received for saving towards specific objectives, such as buying a toy, saving for college, or any other desired item.

Spending Jar: The spending jar is used for discretionary spending on immediate wants or needs. Children can use the money in this jar for small purchases they desire, such as toys, snacks, or any item they wish to buy.

Sharing Jar: The sharing jar is intended for teaching children the value of generosity and giving back. Money placed in this jar is used for charitable donations, helping others in need, or contributing to a cause or charity that resonates with the child.

Through this method, children learn to divide their money into these three categories, gaining an understanding of how to manage funds for different purposes. It instils the habit of allocating money wisely, teaching the importance of saving for future goals, managing spending on immediate desires, and fostering a spirit of generosity by sharing with others.

Moreover, this technique encourages regular conversations about money between parents and children, facilitating discussions on financial goals, budgeting, and responsible financial habits from an early age. The 'Three Jars' method serves as a practical and interactive tool to impart foundational money management skills to children in a clear and tangible way.

Teaching Teens

Teaching teenagers how to handle money is a crucial life skill that sets the stage for their financial well-being in the future. Several effective techniques can impart financial literacy, responsibility, and smart money management to teens, empowering them to make informed financial decisions.

The Compass teaching tool "Two Masters" was specifically designed to teach teens God's way of handling money. Here are some ideas to implement.

1. **Financial Education**: Offering comprehensive financial education is fundamental. Introduce concepts like budgeting, saving, investing, credit, and managing debt through workshops, online resources, or dedicated courses. Practical, real-life examples can help teens grasp these concepts better.

2. **Practical Budgeting Exercises**: Encourage teens to create and maintain budgets. Provide them with a monthly allowance or income based on chores or part-time work. Have them allocate money for various expenses such as

entertainment, savings, and necessities. Tracking spending against this budget fosters financial discipline.

3. **Saving and Goal Setting**: Teach the value of saving by setting achievable financial goals. Whether it's saving for a new phone, a car, or college tuition, establish clear objectives. Encourage regular contributions to savings accounts and discuss the concept of interest and compound growth to underscore the benefits of saving early.

4. **Interactive Learning Tool**s: Utilise interactive tools such as financial apps or online simulations designed for teens. These tools simulate financial scenarios, offering a hands-on approach to learning about investments, expenses, and the consequences of financial decisions.

5. **Practising Smart Spending Habits:** Engage teens in discussions about distinguishing between needs and wants. Encourage comparison shopping, finding discounts, or using coupons to instil the importance of smart spending. Discussions around avoiding impulse purchases and budget-friendly alternatives can be invaluable.

6. **Hands-On Experience:** Encourage teens to take on part-time jobs or internships. Earning their own money provides practical experience in managing income, budgeting, and understanding the value of hard work.

7. **Open Dialogue**: Discuss your financial decisions openly. Encourage questions and maintain an open dialogue about money matters, allowing teens to seek guidance without judgment.

8. **Real-Life Scenarios:** Discuss real-life financial scenarios or case studies relevant to teenagers. Explore topics like student loans, credit card debt, or the impact of interest rates. These discussions prepare them for potential financial challenges they may face in the future.

9. **Encouraging Entrepreneurship:** Nurture an entrepreneurial mindset. Encourage teens to explore their

interests and hobbies that could potentially translate into small business ventures, fostering financial independence and innovation.

By employing these techniques, teens can develop a strong foundation in financial literacy, empowering them to navigate the complexities of personal finance confidently.

Financial Challenges with College-Age

Parenting is a rewarding but challenging journey, and when you have college-age children, a new set of financial responsibilities arises. Transitioning from high school to college is a significant milestone in a young person's life, often with substantial financial challenges. Parents must prepare for these expenses to provide their children with the best opportunities while maintaining their financial stability.

1. **Tuition Costs:** The rising college tuition costs can be overwhelming for parents. Balancing these expenses with other financial priorities can be a significant challenge.
2. **Books and Supplies:** Beyond tuition, there are additional costs for books, supplies, and other educational materials that parents must consider.
3. **Room and Board:** If children live on or near campus, room and board costs can add a substantial financial burden.
4. **Scholarships and Financial Aid:** While these can help, they may not cover all expenses, leaving parents with a financial gap.

Preparing for the Financial Challenges of College-Age
1. **Start Early:** One of the most effective ways to prepare for the financial challenges of college-age children is to start saving early. Consider opening a college savings account.

Consistent contributions over time can help you build a substantial college fund.

2. **Financial Aid and Scholarships**: Encourage your children to explore scholarship opportunities and financial aid options. Research scholarship opportunities that match your child's skills and interests.

3. **Budgeting and Planning:** Help your child understand the importance of budgeting. Teach them to create a budget covering tuition, housing, books, and other essential expenses. This financial literacy will serve them well throughout their college years and beyond.

4. **Part-Time Work and Internships**: Consider encouraging your child to find part-time college internships. These experiences can help cover some expenses and provide valuable professional development.

5. **Communication and Expectations**: Open and honest communication with your son or daughter is essential. Discuss your financial expectations and what you can contribute to their education. Set realistic goals and create a plan together.

6. **Minimise Unnecessary Expenses**: Encourage your child to be mindful of their spending. Avoiding unnecessary expenses and focusing on needs rather than wants can help them maximise their resources.

7. **Use College Resources**: Many colleges offer resources such as work-study programmes, on-campus jobs, and tutoring services. Take advantage of these opportunities to reduce expenses.

8. **Emergency Fund**: Create an emergency fund that can be accessed in case of unexpected expenses or emergencies. This financial safety net can prevent significant disruptions to your child's education.

9. **Insurance Considerations**: Review your insurance policies, such as health and car insurance, to ensure your child's coverage remains adequate while they're away at college.

10. **Supportive Network**: Connect with other parents who have college-age children. Share experiences, tips, and advice for managing college expenses. Building a supportive network can provide valuable insights.

Preparing for the financial challenges of college-age kids requires early planning, open communication, and financial literacy. By starting to save early, exploring financial aid options, and encouraging responsible budgeting, parents can help their children access higher education without sacrificing their financial stability. With the right preparation, families can confidently navigate the college years, knowing they have taken the necessary steps to secure their child's future.

Chapter 12: Tackling financial crises

We live in troubling times, from financial uncertainty to political instability, physical war, and cyber war. Every person faces struggles, whether it is relational, spiritual, or material. Despite the gloom and doom, the Bible gives us hope that we can survive and flourish. Despite our circumstances, we can thrive, grow, multiply, and bear fruit. Our lives can be satisfying and rich in relationships and accomplishments. How, may you wonder? There is an excellent promise in John 16:33, "These things I have spoken to you, so that in Me you may have peace. In the world, you have tribulation, but take courage; I have overcome the world."

Christ is present to work in us and through us to give us an abundant life and experience victory.

The Bible tells of how the disciples were with Jesus in a boat on the Sea of Galilee when a severe storm broke. The disciples were afraid they were going to drown. Jesus was in the back of the boat, sleeping. "Master, save us, we are perishing!"

Jesus challenged them, "Why are you afraid, O you of little faith?" He then calmed the storm.

Beth Moore says, "We want Christ to hurry and calm the storm; He wants us to find Him in the midst of it first. No matter whose fault, God sends us through storms so we can land in a place we never would have otherwise been." [9]

How can we prepare for the storms in life which challenge us to trust in the Lord? God has a part to play, and we have a part to play. I can never do what only He can, but He will not do what we must do. The Lord's role is to control, empower, provide and lead. Our role is to get prepared financially - to build a solid foundation and follow His directions. "The prudent see danger and take refuge, but the simple keep going and suffer for it." (Proverbs 27:12)

We can take steps to build a solid foundation by ...

1. Getting our financial house in order - by putting God's financial principles into practice.
2. Seeking advice - from people who have been through similar situations.
3. Living one day at a time - trusting the Lord in the peace He gives.
4. Being patient - waiting for God's timing.
5. Forgiving - when we are thrust into trouble by people causing our crisis.

Everyone has to go through storms in life, but we don't have to go alone! His activity "will be a shelter and shade from the heat of the day, and a refuge and hiding place from the storm and rain." (Isaiah 4:6). While we may not understand why God allows trials to enter our lives, we thank Him that through them we can come to know who He is.

You can't prevent every difficulty, but you can prepare to survive them by building a solid relationship with the Lord and your partner and improving your finances. The healthier your finances, the better you will be able to cope. The more time you spend getting to know God and what He reveals in the Bible—and applying what you've learned—the better prepared you will be to weather life's storms.

Why do couples get into financial trouble?

Rebecca, recently divorced, said. "My ex and I went to marriage counselling because we fought all the time. When the counsellor asked us what our fights were about, we both said, 'Money!' We could hardly pay the bills. It was tough, and it's what ultimately tore us apart. We couldn't fix our finances, and we couldn't fix our marriage because it was consumed with arguments about money."

A crisis brought on by finances usually involves more than just money. Anger, resentment and hopelessness often take over the relationship. Arguments intensify- or they emotionally withdraw from one another. A crisis can be even more challenging when trust has been broken. One out of every five marriages end because of financial trouble. Often, in a marriage, one partner is more of a spender and one more of a saver. We all have different attitudes to money, generally formed in our youth.
People often react differently to crises. Our experiences, family backgrounds and personalities influence our response to crisis. Some people respond quickly and emotionally, while others are more reflective and require time to sort it out. Some live in denial, while others want to deal with it aggressively.

So, why do couples get into financial trouble? There are both external and internal reasons – and interpersonal reasons.

An external change in economic circumstances can give rise to financial problems. This can result from losing your job, being unable to work due to illness or an accident, or income reduction through economic changes. Financial pressure can come from life milestones like getting married, having children, losing a loved one, separation or retirement. Financial stress can come from unforeseen expenses such as major car repairs or medical expenses.

Internal economic pressure comes from poor money management, such as the lack of budgeting or planning, poor spending habits like impulse buying, and 'retail therapy' to cope with emotional problems or addictions. Debt is a major cause of trouble, whether from internal factors such as lack of contentment, greed, and envy or external factors such as the inability to pay debts due to economic changes.

However, the primary cause of financial trouble in marriage is an inability to adequately communicate about their financial situation. Money problems are rarely about money but arise from deeper, inner problems. Unspoken expectations lead to disappointment and arguments. Envy or jealousy that one partner may earn more than another causes strife. Placing blame or financial power plays can cause massive problems.

Most marriages, if not all, have communication problems! Learning to talk together about issues that affect your relationship is the most critical discipline to grow in a marriage! Talking with God is probably even more strategic for Christian couples in developing healthy finances.

Whatever the reasons, financial pressure and strain on a marriage are real and a significant cause of marriage breakdown.

Coping with financial pressure

How can we become more vital in coping with financial pressures? Here are some steps which we could start to take.

1. Open, effective communication channels – share your financial situation regularly.

2. Accept each other and create safe environments where you can speak the truth without fear.

3. Learn what the Bible says about navigating your finances – join a small group!

4. Adopt biblical principles for economic decision-making (a transparent financial administration, becoming free from debt, learning to be content, setting goals, practising integrity, patience & self-control…)

5. Realise God's unique design for the couple and recognise each other's unique roles in the marriage.

6. Make a spending plan together and have regular 'money dates' to evaluate your finances.

7. Design tools to solve common problems (for example, discuss individual spending above a specific limit, a regular financial evaluation together, use joint accounts)

The husband and wife must support and encourage each other in every way possible during financial troubles.

Times like this can be defining in a relationship—bringing couples closer together or pushing them further apart. It can become the bridge that moves you from pain to a new level of closeness in your marriage. One of the most significant potential benefits is that when people experience a high pain level, they will change. Look at financial problems as God's invitation to learn from Him, improve your communication and navigate your finances – God's way.

Weathering the storms of life

Some storms are resolved quickly; others are chronic. Some reflect the consequences of our actions; others are beyond our control. Some crises impact an entire nation; others are isolated to us as individuals.

A job loss, major illness, birth of a special-needs child, business reversal, death of a family member, identity theft, military deployment, home foreclosure, bankruptcy, or worldwide financial crisis can exert significant pressure on us and our finances. Surveys reveal that many marriages don't survive the stress of these difficulties.

I call these challenges the "storms of life." While some storms amount to little more than a blustery rain shower, others feel like a category-five hurricane.

Please remember this one thing: No matter the crisis, you don't face it alone. Put yourself in the sandals of a few of God's people who faced terrifying category-five storms in the Bible. Job —in a matter of just a few hours—lost his children, his financial resources and ultimately, his health.

Joseph was sold into slavery and thrown into prison. Moses and the children of Israel faced annihilation by Egypt's powerful army at the Red Sea. Daniel was tossed into the lion's den. Paul was beaten, stoned, and left for dead on his missionary journeys. The list goes on and on.

Understanding God's Role in Adversity

In times of crisis, there's nothing more vital than knowing the character of God—His love, care, control, and power. The Bible offers the most profound insight into God's involvement in our challenges, and grasping this truth is essential.

Our understanding of God and His purposes profoundly impacts how we navigate difficulties. If our perception of God is inadequate or distorted, we may struggle to thoroughly embrace and learn from these trials. Moreover, we risk missing out on the peace, contentment, and joy God offers us amid life's storms.

God's Love for You

1 John 4:8 encapsulates the essence of God's nature: "God is love." God's love for you remains constant throughout your life, and He is intimately involved with you as an individual. Psalm 139:17 beautifully illustrates this: "How precious are your thoughts concerning me, O God! How vast is the sum of them! Were I to count them, they would outnumber the grains of sand." In essence, the Creator of the universe is continuously thinking about you!

Contemplate John 15:9, one of the most encouraging verses in the Bible: "As the Father has loved me, so I have loved you." Pause and reflect on the implications of these words. Consider the profound love shared between God the Father and God the Son, which has existed eternally. Jesus affirms that this is how much He loves you!

During a crisis, we must remind ourselves of God's unfailing love and faithfulness. Why? Because adversity can easily lead to discouragement and a loss of hope. It's too familiar to forget God's love and care when difficulties strike, especially when adversity seems relentless.

Jeremiah, a prophet who faced great discouragement, wrote: "I remember my affliction and my wandering, the bitterness...and my soul is downcast within me." (Lamentations 3:19-20) However, he also recalled the Lord's character and declared, "Yet I call this to mind and therefore have hope. Because of the Lord's great love we are not consumed, for his compassions never fail. They are new every morning; great is your faithfulness." (Lamentations 3:21-23)

In times of crisis, it's beneficial to meditate on passages like Hebrews 13:5-6: "God has said, 'Never will I leave you; never will I forsake you.' So we can say with confidence, 'The Lord is my helper; I will not be afraid. What can man do to me?'" and Romans 8:35, 37: "Who shall separate us from the love of Christ? Shall trouble or hardship or persecution or famine or nakedness or danger or sword? ... No, in all these things we are more than conquerors through him who loved us."

Even amid a crisis, the Lord reveals His love and care through acts of kindness. For instance, consider Joseph, who, despite being a slave, found favour with those around him. Genesis 39:3 notes, "[Joseph's] master saw that the Lord was with him." Later, while in prison, "the Lord was with Joseph and extended kindness to him, and gave him favour in the sight of the chief jailer" (Genesis 39:21).

God is in Control

God ultimately controls every event. Numerous passages affirm His sovereignty, such as Psalm 115:3: "Our God is in the heavens; He does whatever He pleases." 1 Chronicles 29:11 reads, "We adore you as being in control of everything." Similarly, Psalm 135:6 states, "Whatever the Lord pleases, He does, in heaven and on earth."

Isaiah 46:10 declares, "My [the Lord's] purpose will stand, and I will do all that I please." Furthermore, Luke 1:37 reassures us, "For nothing will be impossible with God."

Notably, the Lord remains in control even during challenging events. Isaiah 45:6-7 explains, "I am the Lord, and there is no other, the One forming light and creating darkness, causing well-being and creating calamity; I am the Lord who does all these."

God can use adversity.

Consider the Cecropia moth, which emerges from its cocoon after a strenuous struggle to free itself. However, a young boy, attempting to help, carefully cut the cocoon. As a result, the moth's wings were shrivelled and nonfunctional. The boy didn't realise that the moth's struggle to liberate itself was essential to develop its wings and ability to fly.

Similarly, adversity plays a significant role in our lives. God uses difficult and sometimes heartbreaking times to mature us in Christ. James 1:2-4 beautifully expresses this: "Consider it pure joy, my brothers, whenever you face trials of many kinds, because you know that the testing of your faith develops perseverance. Perseverance must finish its work so that you may be mature and complete, not lacking anything."

God designs challenging circumstances for our ultimate benefit. Romans 8:28-29 assures us that "in all things, God works for the good of those who love him, who have been called according to his purpose. For those God foreknew he also predestined to be conformed to the likeness of his Son." The primary good God works in our lives is to make us more like Christ.

Secure Your Financial Foundation

Financial storms can strike anyone, often leaving us bewildered and searching for answers. When faced with these trials, the first question that typically arises is, "How can I solve this problem?" In Matthew 7:24-25, Jesus provides an essential insight: "Everyone who hears these words of mine and puts them into practice is like a wise man who built his house on the rock. The rain came down, the streams rose, and the winds blew and beat against that house; yet it did not fall, because it had its foundation on the rock."

The key to resolving financial problems lies in learning and applying God's principles for handling money. It's that simple yet profoundly transformative. This study holds paramount importance because, upon completing it, you'll grasp God's framework for managing finances. However, understanding is only the first step; application is the second and equally critical step. Navigating the financial storm may require substantial time and effort, but armed with the knowledge of what to do, you can weather it.

James 1:22-25 unequivocally underscores the significance of applying God's wisdom: "Do not merely listen to the word, and so deceive yourselves. Do what it says. Anyone who listens to the word but does not do what it says is like a man who looks in the mirror and, after looking at himself, goes away and immediately forgets what he looks like. But the man who looks intently into the perfect law that gives freedom, and continues to do this, not forgetting what he has heard, but doing it—he will be blessed in what he does."

Never compromise or approach implementation half-heartedly. Follow through with what the Lord has graciously revealed about handling money, and in doing so, you will experience His blessings.

A vital part of this learning process involves embracing a spirit of generosity. During times of financial crisis, the instinct is to clench our resources and become less charitable. However, the Book of Acts provides a different perspective. In Acts 11:28-29, we read about Agabus, a prophet who, through the Spirit, predicted a severe famine. The disciples' immediate response was to open their wallets. Don't let a crisis erode your spirit of generosity. You may not be able to give as much as before, but continue to give.

Swiftly evaluate how the circumstances will affect your financial situation and make necessary adjustments for potentially reduced income or increased expenses. Effective communication is also crucial. Share your thoughts and concerns with the Lord and your spouse. It's vital that scheduling daily times to connect and encourage each other can be transformative. Didie and I have discovered that a crisis doesn't have to weaken our marriage; it can be a catalyst for strengthening it. I firmly believe that God intends for married couples to draw closer during adversity rather than allow it to strain their union.

Never go through a storm alone.

I want to emphasise the importance of not going it alone. Making the wisest decisions in isolation is almost impossible when experiencing a crisis.

Seek advice from people who have been through similar situations. You will draw strength not only from their emotional support but also from their experience. There are people all around you who have weathered severe life storms, and you can gain from their knowledge, learning mistakes to avoid and resources to help. Ask your church and friends to pray; it's their most potent contribution.

Be patient, waiting for God's timing.

Expectations can be damaging during a crisis. When we assume that the Lord will solve our problems in a certain way by a specific time, we set ourselves up for disappointment and frustration.

Someone described patience as accepting a difficult situation without giving God a deadline for removing it. Remember, God's primary purpose in allowing a crisis in the first place is to conform you to Jesus Christ. He is at work in your life and knows exactly how long it will take to produce the results He wants. Ecclesiastes 3:1 says, "There is an appointed time for everything. And there is a time for every event under heaven."

The late Larry Burkett used to say with a smile, "God is seldom early, but He's never late." Be patient. Be careful not to set deadlines for the Lord to act.

Work diligently to solve your problems, with the recognition that you need the moment-by-moment help and counsel of the Lord who loves you. Philippians 4:6-7 is one of my favourite Bible passages when facing difficulties. Every phrase is loaded with meaning. "Be anxious for nothing but in everything by prayer and supplication with thanksgiving let your request be made known to God and the peace of God which surpasses all understanding will guard your heart and mind in Christ Jesus."

Wise Counselor

All couples in crisis will benefit from the counsel of a godly person who can offer objective advice. Some people will panic and make impulsive decisions they regret later. And it is tough to make solid decisions by yourself amid a crisis. Proverbs 19:20 says, "Listen to advice and accept instruction, and in the end, you will be wise."

I like to think of a counsellor as my GPS. Like a wise counsellor, the GPS indicates where you are and how to get where you are going. If you take a wrong turn, the little box starts talking to you. "Turn around," it says. "Take the next right and get back on track."

The best counsellors are concerned people who know Jesus Christ and the Bible well.

Navigating a Marriage Crisis: A Path to Healing

In the face of a marriage crisis, it's essential to evaluate its severity to determine the necessary steps for healing. This process is like assessing an injury; whether you need just a few stitches, require surgery, or even life-saving treatment in a hospital depends on the extent of the injury. Similarly, the gravity of your marital crisis will dictate the course of action.

Depending on the crisis's seriousness, you can choose from three potential options:

1. **Moderate crisis:** Manageable with minor assistance.
2. **Serious crisis:** Requires professional counselling.
3. **Critical crisis:** Demands intervention.

The initial step for a couple is to assess the crisis's severity. During this diagnosis process, it's crucial to maintain love and respect for each other. This will demand courage and humility as you move towards complete honesty. Although honesty can be painful, facing your challenges truthfully is essential, as it is the first step toward healing.

Here's a practical approach to gauge the crisis:

1. **Pray together:** Seek God's wisdom and direction for your situation.

2. **Agree on ground rules:** Establish clear guidelines for addressing the crisis. Ensure that either spouse can call for a time-out to pray together or suspend a discussion if it becomes too intense.

3. **Write letters:** If financial issues have been emotionally charged, writing letters to each other expressing your feelings and identifying the contributing problems can be immensely helpful. Subsequently, come together to pray and discuss the letters.

4. **Identify and confess any sin:** If one spouse is partly responsible for the crisis, confessing the wrongdoing and seeking forgiveness can be healing. True repentance involves "turning away" from the wrongdoing and taking steps to address it, such as seeking help for addiction if that is the root issue.

5. **Search for the underlying cause:** Look beyond the immediate incident to uncover any deep-seated problems that may have been buried for an extended period. Pray for God's guidance to reveal these underlying issues.

6. **Rebuilding the marriage:** Couples recovering from a crisis benefit from community support. Engage with others who

can offer love and hold you accountable for making positive choices. Enrolling in programs like the Navigating Your Finances God's Way small group study has rejuvenated many marriages in just nine weeks, thanks to the encouragement and love provided by fellow participants.

We all need a community of believers who care for us. Solomon wisely notes in Ecclesiastes 4:9-12, "Two are better than one because they have a good return for their work: If one falls down, his friend can help him up. But pity the man who falls and has no one to help him up... Though one may be overpowered, two can defend themselves. A cord of three strands is not quickly broken."

If you or your spouse feels overwhelmed, emotionally hurt, or stuck at any point, you should consider the assistance of a professional marriage counsellor who can facilitate the process. Ensure that the chosen counsellor is a committed Christian with a biblical worldview and experience in handling crises.

For exceptionally fragile marriages that may be at risk of dissolution, more drastic measures are necessary to preserve and mend the union.

Intervention: Saving a Marriage in Crisis

In cases of an acute breakdown in a marriage, intervention becomes necessary, as the couple cannot resolve their issues independently. For intervention to be effective, both spouses must commit to doing whatever it takes to overcome the crisis. This might entail participating in intensive intervention retreats and seeking ongoing marriage counselling.

Selecting the right person or organisation to provide the most effective help. Choosing a trained professional, ideally a mature Christian, such as a pastor, marriage counsellor, or therapist, is advisable. You can identify suitable candidates by seeking referrals from church leadership and conducting online research to discover available resources in your area.

Most severe crises and divorces occur when couples lose hope that anything can be done to restore their marriage. While certain circumstances, like abuse, adultery, or addictions, may lead to inevitable divorce, many problems can be resolved if both partners are dedicated to finding a solution.

Separation and Divorce Considerations

If you are contemplating separation or divorce, it's essential to consider the financial costs involved. If you are already facing financial constraints, these costs can suffocate, as you'll support two households instead of one. Before making a decision that can exacerbate the crisis, carefully evaluate how you will make ends meet and, as far as possible, seek reconciliation. It is never too late!

Go can make a way, where there seems to be no way. Meditate on God's promise in these verses from Isaiah 43:18,19. ""Remember not the former things, nor consider the things of old. Behold, I am doing a new thing; now it springs forth, do you not perceive it? I will make a way in the wilderness and rivers in the desert."

Chapter 13: Preparing for life changes.

Life is constantly changing, and we go through many seasons, each with unique challenges and opportunities. We are either in the middle of it or in transition, and we can be very productive in each season or, if we are not sufficiently prepared, experience significant difficulties.

It is encouraging to realise that, whatever season of life we find ourselves in, "My times are in Your hand …" (Psalm 31:15) My times were formed before I was born and known to the Lord. "Your eyes saw my unformed body; all the days ordained for me were written in your book before one of them came to be. How precious to me are your thoughts, God! How vast is the sum of them!" (Psalm 139:16) The key to sound financial planning for life seasons, is to pray and ask God to reveal His thoughts for the time you find yourselves in.

Life changes

Here are just some common ones:

1. **Married** – or about to get married. Maybe you don't have children yet, or one could be on the way. Saving for a future family is very important.

2. **First Child** – you have brought a gift of life into the world, and everything changes! The fun and games begin! Having a child can bring significant financial change. Maybe one parent or both decide to work less, which decreases income.

3. **Second Child** – Not so great a change as with the first; you're more experienced, but kids can be expensive!

4. **Special needs child** - will change your life and finances in a big way.

5. **Moving home** - a massive upset for the family and a lot of expenses

6. **Children in college** - This is the empty nest season, as kids branch out independently. College costs can be astronomical.

7. **Job loss - or business failure -** brings enormous financial problems and loss of confidence.

8. **Divorce** – with extremely sensitive and complicated financial consequences.

9. **Re-Marriage** – A blended family with new challenges in money management.

10. **Widow/Widower** – So hard to confront, but we must discuss how difficult seasons affect our finances.

11. **Serious Illness** – bringing tough times and unusual financial challenges.

12. **Retirement** - The golden years for which we have to make a sound financial plan.

13. **Bereavement** - when a loved one passes away.

It is important to recognise the season we are in and face the new challenges. The better we have been able to foresee these seasonal changes and plan for them financially, the better we will be equipped to meet the challenges and take advantage of the opportunities they bring.

Talk together about the future, anticipate the seasons you may transition into, and plan your finances well in advance.

Seasons of life

In financial planning, we can generalise the four seasons of life, including accumulation, preservation, distribution and succession. Approaching your finances with these four seasons in mind can help keep you on track toward reaching your long-term financial goals. Each financial season builds on the one before it. Planning each season carefully in advance can help you get the most out of your financial life.

Understanding these four broad "financial seasons" of life can help define where you are today and the next steps you will need to take. Knowing how to handle your money from "season to season" will determine whether you meet or exceed your long-term financial goals.

Spring: Working and Earning Season – ages 20 to 50

Typically, the most extended financial season and time spent accumulating life wealth (not only financial but also physical, relational, productive and spiritual) sets the foundation for your entire life. It's crucial during this stage to set financial goals, evaluate these regularly, and give, save and invest consistently.

Summer: Preservation Season – ages 50 to 65

During this time, you are starting to achieve your long-term goals. Eliminate mortgage and business debt; preserving investments for your retirement is vital while increasing in generosity. Invest in the next generation to help them through college or start businesses.

Autumn: Distribution Season – ages 65+

Prepare for tax liabilities in retirement and how to withdraw from your retirement savings. Many people are blessed to have a 20 to 30-year retirement. Plan your legacy and determine to finish well!

Winter: Succession Season – after death

What do you want to happen to your savings and assets after passing? Without proper planning, it can be eaten up by taxes and fees rather than given to your intended heirs. Your legacy will depend on how well you planned your finances in each of the previous seasons and what estate planning you have prepared in advance.

Preparing Financially for Life Changes

Life is full of changes, and as Christians, we are called to navigate these transitions with wisdom and faith. Financial preparedness is an essential aspect of being responsible stewards of the resources God has entrusted to us. Whether you're preparing for marriage, parenthood, retirement, or any other significant life change, here are some key principles to help you navigate these transitions as a Christian.

1. **Seek God's Guidance**: Before embarking on any financial journey, seeking God's guidance through prayer and reflection is crucial. God's wisdom, as found in the Bible, can provide the foundation for your financial decisions. Proverbs 3:5-6 reminds us to trust in the Lord with all our hearts and lean not on our own understanding. Seek His will in prayer and ask for wisdom and discernment to make sound financial choices.

2. **Evaluate Your Financial Goals:** Having specific goals and regularly adjusting these goals will help you stay focused.

Proverbs 21:5 says, "The plans of the diligent lead to profit as surely as haste leads to poverty." Financial planning requires setting priorities and staying disciplined to achieve them.

3. **Keep adjusting Your Budget:** Proverbs 27:23-27 emphasises the importance of having a plan during changing times: "Be sure you know the condition of your flocks, give careful attention to your herds; for riches do not endure forever, and a crown is not secure for all generations. When the hay is removed and new growth appears and the grass from the hills is gathered in, the lambs will provide you with clothing, and the goats with the price of a field. You will have plenty of goats' milk to feed your family and to nourish your female servants."

4. **Build an Emergency Fund:** Life changes can come with unexpected financial challenges. Building an emergency fund is a way to prepare for these uncertainties. Proverbs 21:20 advises, "In the house of the wise are stores of choice food and oil, but a foolish man devours all he has." An emergency fund is your financial storehouse for unexpected expenses, helping you avoid financial setbacks.

5. **Avoid Debt:** Proverbs 22:7 reminds us, "The rich rule over the poor, and the borrower is slave to the lender." Debt can become a burden that limits your financial freedom. Strive to live within your means and avoid unnecessary debt. Debt-free living provides more flexibility and peace of mind when facing life changes.

6. **Stay Flexible and Trust God:** Lastly, remain flexible in your financial planning. Life changes may not always go as expected, and you may need to adjust your financial strategies. Trust in God's providence and remember that He is ultimately in control. Proverbs 16:3 reminds us to commit our plans to the Lord, and He will establish our paths.

Blended Families

Blended families, where one or both partners bring children from previous relationships into a new household, often face unique financial challenges.

"Emma and John had both experienced the joys and sorrows of marriage before they found each other. With children from their previous unions, they decided to blend their families and start anew. Little did they know that unique financial challenges awaited them.

Emma's three children and John's two came with different financial needs. Emma had been a frugal saver, carefully investing for her children's future. On the other hand, John had spent generously on his children's education and extracurricular activities.

The couple had a heart-to-heart conversation about their finances. Emma worried about her children's future, while John felt the need to provide for his kids in the present. They decided to create a financial plan that addressed both concerns.

Their first step was to establish a shared family budget. They agreed to dedicate some of their income to current expenses, like bills, groceries, and family outings. Another portion would be divided between Emma's and John's children for their needs.

To ensure that each child had equal opportunities, they set up educational funds for all of them. This way, Emma's children could benefit from John's generosity, and John's children could understand the importance of long-term savings.

The couple also introduced their children to the new financial plan. They explained that financial support would be given equally but used differently based on individual needs. Emma's children would use their share for future goals, while John's children would have more immediate access to educational and extracurricular expenses.

Emma and John's love and communication thrived as they learned to navigate the financial complexities of blending two families. They discovered that love could conquer even the most unique financial challenges with open conversations and creative solutions."

Here are some of the financial problems specific to blended families:

1. **Child Support and Alimony Obligations:** One of the most significant financial challenges for blended families is the obligation of child support or alimony payments to the former spouse. These payments can strain the financial resources of the parent making the payments, affecting their ability to contribute to the new household.

2. **Differing Financial Responsibilities:** Blended families may have children with different financial needs. Some children may be grown and financially independent, while others still depend on their parents. This can lead to disparities in financial contributions and responsibilities, causing tension and conflicts.

3. **Estate Planning and Inheritance:** Deciding how to distribute assets and inheritance among biological and stepchildren can be complex. Blended families often require careful estate planning to ensure fair and equitable distribution and avoid potential conflicts among family members.

4. **Coordinating Financial Goals:** Blended families may have different financial goals and priorities. Coordinating these goals can be challenging, especially if one partner has a substantial debt, such as student loans or alimony payments. At the same time, the other is debt-free and focused on saving for retirement or their children's education.

5. **Budgeting for Multiple Households:** Financial planning may need to account for the expenses of maintaining two separate households, mainly when joint custody arrangements

exist. This can result in higher living costs, making budgeting a critical task for the blended family.

6. **Medical and Insurance Expenses:** Decisions about health insurance coverage and medical expenses can be complicated in blended families. Determining which children are covered by a particular health insurance plan and how medical expenses are divided can be contentious.

7. **Complex Tax Implications:** Filing taxes can be more complex for blended families, especially if they have different filing statuses or dependents. Understanding tax laws and potential benefits or consequences is essential for proper financial planning.

8. **Educational Expenses:** Saving for children's education can be complicated when stepchildren are involved. Deciding who will contribute to education funds and to what extent can create financial stress.

9. **Childcare Costs:** Balancing childcare costs for children from different households can be challenging. Decisions about who pays for what, such as extracurricular activities or summer activities, must be made collectively.

10. **Retirement Planning:** Blended families may need to coordinate their retirement plans, such as retirement account contributions and when they plan to retire, to ensure financial security for all family members. This can be complex, especially when considering the potential need to support younger and older children.

Navigating these financial challenges in blended families requires open and honest communication between the partners, careful financial planning, and potentially consulting with financial advisors or family counsellors to find solutions that work for all family members.

Meeting these challenges

1. **Communication**: Open, honest, and regular communication is essential. Discuss financial goals, priorities, and challenges as a family (Proverbs 15:22).
2. **Transparency**: Be transparent about your financial situation. Encourage trust by sharing information about debts, income, and expenses (Ephesians 4:25).
3. **Financial Planning**: Develop a family budget that accommodates the needs of all family members. Plan for both short-term and long-term financial goals (Proverbs 21:5).
4. **Educate and Involve Children**: Teach your children about financial stewardship and involve them in age-appropriate budgeting and decision-making (Proverbs 22:6).
5. **Seek Counsel**: If needed, seek financial advice from a trusted financial advisor or counsellor. Wise counsel can help you make sound financial decisions (Proverbs 15:22).
6. **Savings and Investments**: Plan for the future by saving and investing wisely. Diversify your investments to mitigate risks (Proverbs 13:11).
7. **Grace and Forgiveness**: Quickly extend grace and forgiveness in financial matters. Mistakes can happen, but forgiveness and grace can heal financial wounds (Colossians 3:13).
8. **Reassess and Adjust**: Periodically reassess your financial plan to accommodate changing family dynamics and financial goals. Flexibility is essential for long-term success (Proverbs 16:9).

By cultivating these skills and adopting a collaborative approach to financial matters, blended families can effectively address and resolve their unique financial challenges, promoting harmony and financial well-being within the family unit.

Financial Consequences of One Partner Losing Their Job

A marriage is profoundly impacted when one partner loses their job. This unexpected twist can send ripples through a relationship, affecting the couple's finances and emotional well-being. What are the consequences of one partner losing their job?

"Paul and Susan had built a life full of dreams and shared ambitions. They were a close-knit couple, and their love had seen them through many joys and challenges. However, when Susan lost her job unexpectedly, they faced a financial crisis that tested their bond.

The loss of Susan's job was a shock. She had been the primary breadwinner, and her income had covered a significant portion of their expenses. With bills piling up, they realised they were suddenly living on one income, and it was a struggle to make ends meet.

As the weeks turned into months, the strain on their finances began to affect their marriage. They argued about money more often, and the stress weighed heavily on them. Paul tried to pick up extra work to compensate for the loss of Susan's income, but the financial gap remained.

Their emergency savings quickly dwindled, and they began to rely on credit cards to cover essential expenses. The mounting debt added to their worries, and they felt trapped in a cycle of financial stress.

Paul and Susan knew they had to take action. They started by creating a strict budget, cutting back on non-essential expenses, and seeking financial advice. Susan also actively searched for new job opportunities, networking and applying to positions in her field.

Through this challenging period, Paul and Susan learned to lean on each other for emotional support. Their love and commitment were a source of strength, helping them navigate the financial crisis together. They discovered the importance of open communication, understanding, and teamwork in overcoming such challenges."

Effects of unemployment on marriage

1. **Financial Strain:** Financial strain is one of the most immediate consequences of a partner losing their job. The loss of a steady income can disrupt the couple's budget and lead to difficulties in covering daily expenses. Couples should work together to revise their budget, cut back on non-essential expenses, and seek additional sources of income if possible. Addressing financial issues as a team can help prevent disagreements and reduce stress.

2. **Emotional Impact:** Losing a job can be emotionally devastating. The partner who loses their job may experience feelings of inadequacy, frustration, and even depression. This emotional turmoil can affect their self-esteem and overall well-being. Both partners need to offer emotional support during this challenging time. Encouragement, understanding, and reassurance can go a long way in helping them through this challenging period.

3. **Changes in Roles and Responsibilities:** When one partner loses their job, the dynamics in the relationship can shift. The partner who remains employed may feel an increased sense of responsibility, both financially and in terms of household duties. This change in roles can lead to stress and a sense of imbalance. Couples can address this consequence by openly discussing their evolving roles. They can work together to redistribute responsibilities and share the burden of maintaining the household.

4. **Impact on Future Plans:** The loss of a job can also impact a couple's future plans. Financial instability can delay or alter these goals, whether saving for a house, planning a family,

or pursuing further education. In uncertain times, couples can develop their trust in the Lord's provision of their needs.

Facing the challenge

.Here are some Biblical principles that can provide guidance and support during this difficult time:

1. **Trust in God's Provision**: Place your trust in God's provision, knowing He is your ultimate source of security and sustenance. Seek His guidance and trust in His plan (Philippians 4:19).

2. **Prayer and Supplication**: Turn to prayer as a source of strength and comfort. Pray together as a couple, seeking God's wisdom, guidance, and peace during unemployment (Philippians 4:6-7).

3. **Support and Encouragement**: Encourage and support your spouse emotionally and spiritually. Be a source of comfort and strength as you face the challenges together (1 Thessalonians 5:11).

4. **Open Communication**: Maintain open and honest communication about the situation. Discuss financial concerns, fears, and plans. Develop a budget and financial plan that accommodates the changes (Proverbs 15:22).

5. **Willingness to Adapt**: Be willing to adapt to the changing circumstances. It may require adjustments in your lifestyle and spending habits to make ends meet during this period (Philippians 4:12).

6. **Contentment**: Cultivate contentment with your current situation, recognising that God provides for your needs. Avoid unnecessary comparison or coveting what others have (Hebrews 13:5).

7. **Networking and Community**: Utilize your personal and professional networks to explore job opportunities. Lean on

your church and community for support and guidance (Proverbs 15:22).

8. **Patience**: Exercise patience in the job search process. Recognise that it may take time to find the right opportunity. Trust in God's timing and remain hopeful (Psalm 27:14).

9. **God's Guidance**: Remain open to the possibility that God may have a new path or direction for your career. Be receptive to His guidance and leading (Proverbs 3:5-6).

10. **Gratitude**: Maintain an attitude of gratitude for the blessings you have, even in challenging times. Count your blessings and recognise God's faithfulness (1 Thessalonians 5:18).

By applying these Biblical principles, a couple facing the challenge of job loss can find strength, support, and guidance to navigate this difficult season with faith and unity. Facing the consequences of job loss together can strengthen a marriage, ultimately reinforcing the bond between partners. Through open communication, empathy, and collaborative problem-solving, couples can weather the storm and emerge from this trial with a more profound sense of resilience and love.

Preparing for the Unexpected Through Saving

Life is replete with unexpected financial expenses, crises, health issues, job loss, etc. Saving for the unexpected is a tangible way to heed this advice. It allows us to weather life's storms without being overwhelmed by them.

Unexpected expenses can lead to financial, emotional, and health-related consequences. To avoid these pitfalls, it's crucial to establish an emergency fund or savings specifically designated for unforeseen circumstances.

"Sarah and David, a couple deeply in love, enjoyed a stable and harmonious life. However, they had unwittingly overlooked a crucial aspect of financial security: preparing for unexpected expenses. This omission would soon test their relationship's strength and financial stability.

An unexpected car breakdown overshadowed their initial bliss. A hefty repair bill made them panic, exposing their lack of an emergency fund. The subsequent high-interest credit card debt set the stage for financial setbacks. What had begun as a minor car repair issue had snowballed into a relentless cycle of debt.

Sarah and David's financial difficulties began to erode their relationship, causing more frequent and heated arguments. Their credit card debt and rising interest payments felt like a weight they couldn't shake off. The initial illusion of financial stability had crumbled, leaving them anxious, worried, and trapped in a cycle of economic turmoil."

Uncertainty is the thread that runs through every individual's journey. The Bible teaches us valuable lessons about stewardship, foresight, and preparedness. "The prudent sees danger and hides himself, but the simple go on and suffer for it." (Proverbs 22:3)

The Consequences of Not Saving for Unexpected Expenses

While focusing on our regular bills and immediate financial goals is easy, failing to save for unforeseen expenses can have profound consequences. Let's delve into what happens when we don't prepare for life's curveballs.

1. **Financial Stress and Anxiety:** One of the most immediate consequences of not saving for unexpected expenses is increased financial stress and anxiety. When an unforeseen bill or emergency arises, and there's no cushion in savings, it can lead to sleepless nights, strained relationships, and a constant feeling of being on the edge.

2. **Mounting Debt:** Many people turn to credit cards or loans when they haven't saved for such situations to cover

unexpected expenses. While these options provide temporary relief, they often result in mounting debt due to high interest rates and fees.

3. **Selling Assets:** Without an emergency fund or savings set aside for unexpected expenses, you might sell assets to cover the costs. This could mean parting with valuable possessions or assets like your car or home. Selling assets hastily often leads to emotional distress.

4. **Borrowing from Friends and Family:** Another coping mechanism when unprepared for unexpected expenses is borrowing from friends and family. While loved ones may provide help, this can strain relationships and lead to feelings of guilt or dependence.

5. **Impact on Mental and Physical Health:** The stress and anxiety resulting from unpreparedness for unexpected expenses can significantly impact your mental and physical health. The constant worry about how to cover unforeseen costs can lead to sleep disturbances, increased blood pressure, and even depression.

Importance of saving for the unexpected

The Bible gives important perspectives on guiding us to a prosperous future.

1. The Parable of the Wise Steward

The master commends his servant and rewards him for his wisdom. "And the Lord said, 'Who then is the faithful and wise manager, whom his master will set over his household, to give them their portion of food at the proper time? Blessed is that servant whom his master will find so doing when he comes.'" - Luke 12:42-43 (ESV)

Saving for the unexpected is an act of stewardship that reflects our commitment to being prepared for the future, just as the wise servant was.

2. Joseph's Example of Prudent Saving

Joseph interpreted Pharaoh's dream about seven years of plenty followed by seven years of famine. He recommended storing grain during the years of plenty to prepare for the famine ahead.

"Now therefore let Pharaoh select a discerning and wise man, and set him over the land of Egypt. Let Pharaoh proceed to appoint overseers over the land and take one-fifth of the produce of the land of Egypt during the seven plentiful years." - Genesis 41:33-34 (ESV)

Joseph's foresight and diligent saving ensured the survival of his family and the people of Egypt during the famine.

3. Proverbs: A Wealth of Wisdom

The book of Proverbs is a treasure trove of wisdom on various aspects of life, including finances. Proverbs 6:6 asks us to follow the ant's example. "Go to the ant, you sluggard; consider its ways and be wise! It has no commander, no overseer or ruler, yet it stores its provisions in summer and gathers its food at harvest." (Proverbs 6:6-8) This verse underscores the value of saving for the future and guarding against wasteful spending in uncertain times.

In conclusion, the Bible provides profound insights into saving for the unexpected. By embracing these principles, we demonstrate faithfulness and wisdom in our financial management and equip ourselves to navigate the uncertainties of life with confidence and grace. Saving for the unexpected is not merely a financial act; it's a testament to our commitment to being responsible stewards of the blessings we've received.

A well-funded emergency fund provides peace of mind, financial stability, and the ability to face life's surprises with confidence and resilience. By taking the initiative to save for the unexpected, you're securing your financial future and your overall well-being.

Seek Counsel

The Bible emphasises the importance of seeking advice in financial matters and beyond. Proverbs 19:20 wisely counsels, "Listen to advice and accept instruction, and in the end, you will be wise" (NIV). When seeking counsel, your spouse should be your first and most trusted confidant.

As an independent, strong-willed businessman, I struggled to turn to my wife for financial guidance in the early years of our marriage. I wrongly believed that her lack of formal financial training made her input less valuable. However, as time passed, I realised that her wisdom often saved us a lot of money.

Men tend to gravitate towards a factual approach, while women often possess a keen, intuitive nature that proves remarkably accurate. This blend of perspectives enables couples to strike a harmonious balance in their decision-making. I believe the Lord honours the wife's role as a helper to her husband, frequently using her to communicate crucial insights.

Husbands, take heed: no matter your wife's financial background, her counsel is invaluable. I made a personal commitment never to make significant financial decisions without my wife's agreement, and it has rescued us from financial pitfalls on more than one occasion.

Agreeing on financial decisions is vital because both spouses will face the consequences, be they positive or negative. Even if their choice proves disastrous, agreeing protects their relationship by leaving no grounds for an "I told you so" response.

This unity shields the relationship and conveys a message of love and respect, affirming the value of each other's insights. When a couple seeks each other's advice, they actually are communicating, "I love you. I value your insight.".

Chapter 14: Preparing for the golden years.

It is a known fact that retirement and death are two life realities that we least enjoy talking about and are primarily ill-prepared for.

Of unfathomable comfort to the Christian is the truth that both of these have been fully covered and provided for in the death and resurrection of the Lord Jesus Christ.

I find these words of His most comforting: "Therefore, do not worry about tomorrow, for tomorrow will worry about itself. Each day has enough trouble of its own"; and "In my Father's house are many rooms; if it were not so, I would have told you. I am going there to prepare a place for you. And if I go and prepare a place for you, I will come back and take you to be with me that you also may be where I am. You know the way to the place to where I am going." (Matthew 6:34 and John 14:2-4)

These great promises, however, do not mean that we must ignore our responsibility of planning for the future so that we honour God in the way we prepare for the realities of retirement and death. Estate planning and preparing a Will can be daunting, but it is nevertheless vital.

It is essential to give due thought and consideration to your financial and estate planning and decide what actions to take. Procrastination, putting off doing anything, is all too common. There are many reasons for this. Some are unwilling to face the fact that we will all, one day, 'graduate' and feel that planning for their death forces them to acknowledge this. Others think they have too little to be bothered with or that they cannot find the time to address the issue of planning when they are unlikely to die for years yet.

One common reason for not taking action is that couples struggle to agree on what to do. That is often the case for those who have children from an earlier marriage - a blended family. One spouse might feel his or her children should inherit their wealth, and not the ex's. Thus, money can become a marital problem, and to avoid arguments, they ignore the issue, leaving it to be sorted out by others after they die as an easy way out of this problem.

Plan for the Golden Years

Widows share a common concern—financial fear and uncertainty. In their time of grief, they frequently find themselves at a loss, not knowing whom to trust or how to manage their finances. Some even harbour feelings of anger, wishing their late husbands had taken the time to put their financial affairs in order.

Both partners must be prepared for the eventuality of one partner's passing. This preparedness involves understanding how to handle financial matters, having sufficient life insurance to replace the primary breadwinner's income, and having a complete understanding of their assets and debts. Equally important is the need to personally know and trust the financial advisors who will guide you.

Remarkably, statistics reveal that around seven out of every ten individuals pass away without a will, leaving their state to determine the distribution of their assets. Avoid this scenario to spare your surviving spouse from complicated legal procedures, increased expenses, and potentially higher taxes. In some unfortunate circumstances, the court may even appoint a guardian who may not share your Christian beliefs to raise your children if you haven't specified your wishes in your will.

Remember that approximately 36% of individuals pass away before reaching retirement age. Therefore, don't delay preparing your will, even if you're relatively young. An alternative to the traditional will is a revocable living trust, but seeking legal counsel is essential to determine which option is more suitable for your specific circumstances.

Setting Your House in Order

"In those days, Hezekiah became ill and was at the point of death. The prophet Isaiah son of Amoz went to him and said, "This is what the LORD says: Put your house in order because you are going to die; you will not recover." (Isaiah 38:1)

Setting your house in order, in preparation for the inevitable, is a thoughtful and responsible act. Here's a checklist to guide you:

1. **Organise Important Documents:** Compile essential documents, including your will, insurance policies, bank statements, birth and marriage certificates and property deeds in one accessible place.

2. **Clear Communication:** Discuss your wishes openly with family members, ensuring everyone knows your decisions and plans.

3. **Create a Will:** Clearly outline how you want your assets distributed, ensuring your wishes are legally documented.

4. **Appoint an Executor:** Designate someone you trust to fulfil your wishes and manage your affairs after your passing.

5. **Life Insurance Review:** Ensure your life insurance policy is up-to-date and provides adequate coverage for your loved ones.

6. **Digital Estate Plan:** Specify how you want your online accounts handled, from social media to financial platforms.

7. **Healthcare Directives:** Draft a living will and designate a healthcare proxy to make medical decisions if you cannot.

8. **Funeral Arrangements:** Outline your funeral or memorial service preferences, reducing the burden on grieving loved ones.

9. **Financial Review:** Consolidate and document your financial accounts, investments, and outstanding debts.

10. 1**Beneficiary Updates:** Regularly review and update beneficiaries on insurance policies, retirement accounts, and other assets.

11. **Power of Attorney:** Designate someone to manage your financial affairs if incapacitated.

12. **Debt Management:** Develop a plan for settling outstanding debts, preventing financial burdens on your estate.

Taking these steps ensures a smoother transition for your loved ones and gives you peace of mind that your affairs are in order.

Compass offers a useful small group experience to help you through the process of setting your house in order.

Is Retirement a Biblical Goal?

In our culture, retirement is often portrayed as the ultimate goal—a time of leisure and relaxation. But is this a goal aligned with biblical principles? In the parable of the rich fool, Jesus strongly challenges the idea of a life of ease and self-indulgence: He exclaimed, "I will say to my soul, 'Soul, you have many goods laid up for many years to come; take your ease, eat, drink, and be merry.' But God said to him, 'You fool!'" (Luke 12:19-20).

While there is a place for leisure and relaxation, making it the primary focus of life can be detrimental. The Bible acknowledges the importance of leisure and emphasises the need for balance.

As long as we are physically and mentally capable, there is no biblical basis for retiring and becoming unproductive. Aging should not be a reason to stop fulfilling the work that God has called us to. He provides the strength and wisdom necessary to continue serving Him.

Instead of traditional retirement, the Bible suggests transitioning to a different type or intensity of labour as we age, potentially focusing on mentoring and imparting wisdom to younger generations. This season of life allows us to utilise the experience and insights gained over a lifetime.

If we are financially secure and no longer dependent on our careers for sustenance, we may shift our focus from work to serving others as God leads us.

Hans, who dropped out of college and built a successful business, initially intended to retire early and enjoy a life of leisure. However, after studying the principles we're discussing, he felt compelled to reevaluate his plans. He prayed for God's guidance and, instead of retiring, decided to build businesses that would financially support the work of Christ. His goal is for these enterprises to contribute regularly to ministry efforts.

While Hans's vision may seem ambitious, what's undeniable is his newfound sense of purpose and engagement in walking by faith with Christ. He's significantly impacting his employees and supporting global ministries serving vulnerable women and children.

How many Christians set their sights on a "Sabbath evening" of life—resting, playing, travelling, etc.—the world's substitute for heaven since the world does not believe that there will be a heaven beyond the grave? The mindset of our peers is that we must reward ourselves now in this life for the long years of our labour. Eternal rest and joy after death are irrelevant considerations. When you don't believe in heaven to come, and you are not content in the glory of Christ now, you will seek the kind of retirement that the world seeks. But what a strange reward for a Christian to set his sights on! Twenty years of leisure (!) while living in the midst of the Last Days of infinite consequence for millions of people who need Christ. What a tragic way to finish the last mile before entering the presence of the King, who finished his last mile so differently! "John Piper [10]

Preparing for Retirement

Retirement is a significant milestone in our journey through life, and it carries great importance from a financial and spiritual perspective. Retirement, often viewed as a time of rest and reflection, should also be when we apply biblical wisdom and stewardship to our financial well-being.

"Tom and Susan had always looked forward to their retirement years. As they approached their late 50s, they imagined leisurely strolls on sunlit beaches, exploring distant lands and cherishing the moments they'd longed for throughout their working lives. However, a sobering realisation struck them as retirement age drew near - they hadn't prepared financially for this new chapter.

Sitting at their kitchen table, Tom and Susan reviewed their financial statements. They realised they had saved far less than they had initially envisioned. Years of occasional splurges, a few unexpected expenses, and a lack of disciplined savings had left them with a retirement account that fell significantly short of their retirement goals.

Their comfortable home, once a symbol of success, now seemed like an anchor, tethering them to a mortgage they could no longer afford if they stopped working. The dream of travelling and exploring new places felt more distant than ever.

One evening, as they watched the sunset from their porch, Tom turned to Susan and said, "We've always wanted to travel and enjoy our retirement, but it seems like we haven't saved enough."

Susan nodded in agreement, her expression reflecting a mix of disappointment and determination. "We may not be able to retire as early as we'd hoped, but we can still make a plan. Let's start by cutting unnecessary expenses and exploring part-time work opportunities."

With a newfound determination, Tom and Susan overhauled their financial approach. They cut back on discretionary spending, downsized to a smaller home, and began contributing more to their retirement accounts.

Tom and Susan learned the importance of financial planning, discipline, and adaptability. They discovered it's never too late to take control of your financial future. The delayed retirement gave them a renewed sense of purpose and determination to make the most of their golden years.

As they finally retired in their early 70s, they embarked on new adventures, both near and far. They may not have achieved early retirement, but they found that their journey was enriched by the lessons they learned and the second chance they had to create the retirement they had always dreamed of.

Making a Financial Plan for Retirement

1. **Stewardship: Managing God's Resources**: The Bible teaches us about stewardship, the responsible and faithful management of the resources that God has entrusted to us. Our finances are among these resources, and Proverbs 27:23-24 provides valuable insight: "Know well the condition of your flocks, and give attention to your herds, for riches do not last forever; and does a crown endure to all generations?" These verses underscore the importance of diligent oversight of our financial affairs. Creating a financial retirement plan manifests this stewardship, ensuring we manage our resources wisely and responsibly, even later.

2. **Providing for Your Household:** The Bible reminds us of our responsibility to provide for our families. "Anyone who does not provide for their relatives, and especially for their own household, has denied the faith and is worse than an unbeliever." (1 Timothy 5:8) Retirement planning isn't merely about securing your future; it's also about maintaining your ability to provide for your family. By creating a financial plan, you uphold your commitment to care for your loved ones, ensuring their financial stability during retirement.

3. **Preparing for the Future:** The Bible encourages us to prepare for the future. "The plans of the diligent lead to profit as surely as haste leads to poverty." (Proverbs 21:5). This verse underscores the significance of prudent and deliberate planning. By establishing a financial retirement plan, you are safeguarding your future and averting financial burdens on your family and society as a whole.

4. **Giving Back to the Community**: Retirement is not just an opportunity for personal enjoyment; it's also a season for giving back to the community and supporting charitable

causes. " Each of you should give what you have decided in your heart to give, not reluctantly or under compulsion, for God loves a cheerful giver. And God is able to bless you abundantly, so that in all things at all times, having all that you need, you will abound in every good work.." (2 Corinthians 9:7,8). A well-structured retirement plan enables you to allocate resources to support those in need and positively impact the world. Whether through charitable donations, volunteer work, or mentoring the next generation, retirement provides the time and means to be a cheerful giver.

5. **Peace of Mind**: One of the most valuable aspects of financial planning for retirement is the peace of mind it offers. Proverbs 15:22 (NIV) wisely tells us, "Plans fail for lack of counsel, but with many advisers, they succeed." Seeking counsel from financial experts and creating a retirement plan ensures you can confidently enter your retirement years. Knowing that you've made thoughtful and informed decisions about your financial future, you can have peace of mind.

By embracing Biblical stewardship, providing for your household, preparing for the future, giving back to the community, and finding peace of mind, you create a financial plan that aligns with God's teachings and ensures a prosperous and purposeful retirement. So, take the time to develop your retirement plan and step into your golden years with a retirement plan that will be a testament to faithful stewardship and a time of joyful giving.

Estate planning

An organised estate is one of the most precious gifts you can leave your spouse during the Golden Years.

Martin and Leanne were deeply committed to each other and their children, but like many, they never thought much about

estate planning. They were too busy enjoying life's adventures. Years passed, and they built a beautiful life together, with a lovely home, successful careers, and a growing family. However, tragedy can strike when least expected. One fateful day, Martin passed away suddenly due to an unforeseen accident. The grief that washed over Leanne and their children was immeasurable.
But what made the situation even more challenging was the lack of proper estate planning. Martin and Leanne had never discussed what should happen in the event of one of their deaths. No will, power of attorney, or clear instructions about their assets existed.

This lack of planning led to a myriad of complications. The family had to navigate through a complex, emotionally and financially draining legal process. Leanne struggled to access the family's bank accounts and was uncertain about the fate of their home. The children faced uncertainty about their future, which was overwhelming during an already difficult time.

Leanne realised the consequences of not paying attention to estate planning. It added stress and resulted in substantial financial losses due to taxes and legal fees. Their dreams of providing a secure future for their children seemed to be slipping away.

The story of Martin and Leanne serves as a poignant reminder of the importance of estate planning. They could have spared their family from unnecessary hardships if they had planned and communicated their wishes. Their love could have continued to shine through even in their absence.

Ultimately, their story teaches us that estate planning is not just about finances; it's about securing the future for your loved ones. Start early, have those vital conversations, and make a plan to ensure that your legacy is one of love, care, and support for the ones you cherish the most. Like Martin and Leanne, let us all be inspired to take action and protect our family's future with wisdom and foresight.

Though it may sound like a modern financial concept, estate planning has deep roots in the teachings of the Bible. The Scriptures provide valuable guidance on managing our earthly possessions and providing for our loved ones, emphasising principles that extend far beyond material wealth.

1. **Stewardship**: The Bible teaches us that everything we have belongs to God. We are merely stewards of the resources entrusted to us during our time on Earth. This perspective should underpin our estate planning efforts. Recognising our role as stewards encourages us to manage our assets responsibly, ensuring they are used for the benefit of others, especially our family.

2. **Provision for Family**: Our family should be provided for, not just while we are alive but also after our passing. Estate planning allows us to make provisions for our loved ones, ensuring their well-being.

3. **Legacy of Generosity**: The Bible encourages us to be generous and leave a legacy of benevolence. Incorporating charitable giving into your estate plan can be a powerful way to leave a lasting impact on causes that matter to you.

4. **Wise Stewardship of Resources**: Through estate planning, we can ensure that our assets are distributed according to our wishes and in a manner that reflects responsible stewardship.

5. **Avoiding Strife**: Fights over inheritances and assets among family members are sadly common. The Bible advises against such conflicts. Proverbs 17:14 says, "The beginning of strife is like letting out water, so quit before the quarrel breaks out." Estate planning can help prevent such disputes by providing a clear and well-documented distribution plan.

6. **Healthcare and End-of-Life Decisions**: Planning for healthcare and end-of-life decisions is crucial to estate planning. The Bible encourages us to consider issues related to

our well-being, such as honouring our parents and making choices aligned with our faith.

7. **Contentment**: A recurring theme in the Bible is contentment. Contentment helps us focus on what truly matters rather than amassing wealth. In estate planning, the emphasis should be on providing for essential needs and ensuring the well-being of family members rather than amassing extravagant wealth.

When a marriage partner passes away without making a will, it can lead to a series of complex legal, financial, and emotional challenges. Creating a will is not just a matter of asset distribution; it's a way to provide clarity, security, and peace of mind to the surviving spouse and family, ensuring that the deceased partner's wishes are respected and minimising the potential for disputes and complications during an already emotionally taxing time.

In Genesis 49, before his death, Jacob made clear and specific instructions regarding distributing his possessions among his sons. This act reflects the biblical principle of fairness and clarity in estate planning. A well-structured will helps avoid disputes among heirs and ensures your wishes are respected.

Sally and Derek were a loving couple who had shared their lives, dreams, and laughter for decades. They had built a beautiful life together, nurtured a family, and enjoyed their companionship. However, neither had ever considered the importance of making a will.

Tragedy struck one fateful day when Derek, the pillar of their family, unexpectedly passed away. Grief washed over Sally, leaving her heartbroken and overwhelmed. As she began to grapple with her loss, the realisation struck that Derek had left no will behind to guide her through the complexities of managing their shared life.

Without a will, their world soon descended into chaos. Sally had to navigate a legal process to access Derek's accounts, assets, and property. The absence of a clear distribution plan left her anxious and unsure about their family's financial future.

Tensions rose among family members as they grappled with the uncertainties of asset distribution. Relatives had different interpretations of Derek's intentions, leading to conflicts that further strained Sarah's emotional state.

As the days turned into weeks and the legal processes stretched on, Sally understood the profound consequences of their failure to make a will. She had to endure prolonged emotional turmoil and financial stress, all of which could have been alleviated with a simple document outlining their wishes.

In this poignant story, Sally and Derek's experience serves as a sobering reminder of the importance of estate planning. It demonstrates how a seemingly small oversight, like not creating a will, can have profound and lasting repercussions on the lives of those left behind. Their story teaches us that love and responsibility extend beyond our lifetime and that making a will is a meaningful way to protect and provide for the ones we cherish.

The importance of estate planning and creating a will is not just about managing assets; it's about being good stewards, providing for the family, demonstrating generosity, and ensuring fair and wise resource management. A well-crafted will aligns with these principles, allowing you to leave a legacy that reflects your faith and values while providing for the well-being of your loved ones.

When a marriage partner passes away without making a will, it can create a host of unintended and often overwhelming challenges for the surviving spouse and their family. The absence of a will leaves critical matters up to legal processes and the default rules of intestate succession, which can vary significantly depending on the jurisdiction.

1. **Uncertainty in Asset Distribution**: One of the most immediate consequences is uncertainty about how the deceased partner's assets will be distributed. In many cases, the surviving spouse may not understand what they are entitled to, and this lack of clarity can lead to disputes among heirs.
2. **Complex Legal Procedures**: Settling the deceased partner's estate can become a complicated legal ordeal involving probate courts, lawyers, and lengthy proceedings. This can prolong the grieving process and add to the surviving spouse's stress and emotional burden.
3. **Financial Strain**: Without access to the deceased partner's assets and accounts, the surviving spouse may struggle to cover immediate financial needs, such as funeral expenses, mortgage payments, and bills.
4. **Potential for Disputes:** The absence of a will can lead to disagreements among family members about the distribution of assets. Inheritance disputes can strain relationships and create further emotional turmoil during an already trying time.
5. **Tax Implications**: The lack of estate planning can result in higher tax liabilities for the surviving spouse and heirs. Proper estate planning can minimise these tax burdens.
6. **Guardianship Issues**: If the couple had children, the absence of a will can complicate decisions about guardianship. The court may have to step in to determine who will care for the children, a decision that may not align with the deceased partner's wishes.
7. **Protecting Your Children's Well-being:** If something happens to both parents, a will is the only legally recognised way to express your wishes regarding who should care for your children. Without a will, the court will make this crucial decision without your input, potentially placing your children in a less-

than-ideal situation. Creating a will to ensure guardianship for your children is of paramount importance for several significant reasons:

a. **Maintaining Family Continuity:** Your will allows you to choose a guardian who can provide your children with a stable and loving environment. This choice ensures that your children can continue to be part of the same family, maintaining their relationships with extended family members, which can be vital for their emotional well-being.

b. **Avoiding Family Conflicts:** Without a clear designation in your will, disagreements may arise among family members regarding who should have custody of your children. These disputes can be emotionally taxing for your children, who may witness conflicts during a difficult time.

c. **Aligning with Your Values**: A will allows you to select a guardian who shares your values, beliefs, and parenting philosophies. This ensures that your children will be raised in an environment that aligns with your wishes and provides a consistent upbringing.

d. **Legal Protection**: A properly executed will provide a legally binding document that clearly states your intentions. This can help prevent any challenges to your guardianship decisions, as it represents your explicit wishes regarding the care of your children.

e. **Minimising Court Involvement:** With a will in place, the court's role is typically limited to confirming your designated guardian, making the process smoother and less time-consuming. The court's involvement can become a protracted legal process without a will.

f. **Peace of Mind:** Creating a will to ensure guardianship for your children offers you peace of mind. It allows you to take control of an essential aspect of your children's future, knowing that their well-being and upbringing are secured according to your wishes.

In essence, a will allows you to make one of the most critical decisions in your children's lives—choosing their guardian. It ensures that your children will be cared for by someone you trust, who shares your values and can provide a stable and loving environment. While the thought of not being there for your children is complex, creating a will is a responsible and caring step to protect their future and well-being

Bereavement

In the wake of losing a marriage partner, the profound emotional pain is often accompanied by significant financial challenges. The financial consequences can be overwhelming, but finding solace in biblical wisdom can provide a steady guiding light through the darkest times.

"John and Mary had weathered many storms together. Their love was unwavering; they had built a life filled with cherished memories for years. But when Mary fell seriously ill, their world was turned upside down.

Mary's long illness demanded extensive medical treatment and care. As her condition worsened, John became her primary caregiver, never leaving her side. He had to take an extended leave from work, and without his income, they relied on their savings to cover medical bills and everyday expenses. The strain on their finances was palpable.

When Mary's battle with illness came to a heart-wrenching end, John was left with not only profound grief but also severe financial consequences. The medical bills, despite insurance, had accumulated to a staggering sum. Funeral expenses added to the burden. The loss of Mary's income and the fact that John's career had been put on hold had left them financially vulnerable.

John found himself navigating a complex web of financial challenges. The mortgage payments were at risk, and everyday expenses were a constant worry. He felt the weight of debt and the threat of foreclosure. The life he and Mary had built together was now in jeopardy.

While the emotional pain of losing Mary was immeasurable, John also grappled with the stress of the financial crisis. The burden of debt, compounded by the loss of his wife's income, was overwhelming. He was faced with difficult decisions about their home and future financial stability.

In the face of such a tragic loss and the dire financial consequences that followed, John sought support from friends and family. He also contacted financial advisors to explore options for managing the debt and safeguarding their home.

Mary's passing had left a profound void in John's life, and the financial challenges that came with it were a formidable mountain to climb. Yet, in their shared love and memory, John found the strength to face this crisis head-on, determined to honour Mary's legacy and protect the life they had built together."

Assessing the Financial Impact of Bereavement

The death of a marriage partner often translates to a sudden and substantial loss of income. Whether the departed spouse was the primary breadwinner or a contributing partner to the household finances, their absence directly impacts the surviving spouse's financial stability. It's imperative to assess the financial impact comprehensively, considering immediate expenses, ongoing financial obligations, and long-term goals. The first step toward charting a new course is clearly understanding the financial landscape.

Relying on God's Provision: Biblical teachings remind us of God's role as our provider. In Matthew 6:25-26, Jesus urges us to consider the birds of the air and how God cares for them. He reassures us that if God cares for the birds, He will certainly care for us. This verse is a powerful reminder that our trust should rest in God's provision in times of financial distress. It encourages us not to be anxious about our needs, knowing that our faith can provide comfort during financial trials.

Seeking Support from Your Church Community: The Bible emphasises the importance of community and coming together in times of need. Acts 2:44-45 tells us about the early Christian community, which shared their possessions to support one another. You can often find emotional support, guidance, and sometimes even financial assistance in your church or faith community. It's essential not to hesitate to reach out to your fellow believers in need. The strong bonds within your faith community can provide solace and aid in navigating financial challenges.

Creating a New Financial Plan: Once the financial impact has been assessed and you've sought support from your faith community, it's time to create a new financial plan. This plan should encompass a budget that reflects your changed financial circumstances. It should address immediate expenses and long-term financial goals, considering housing, debt management, and savings. Crafting a financial roadmap that aligns with your current reality is crucial in regaining financial stability and control.

Exploring Financial Assistance: The Bible encourages us to seek wisdom and help from others. Proverbs 15:22 advises us to seek counsel, and there's no shame in exploring financial assistance options. This may include survivor's benefits, insurance policies, or financial aid from charitable organisations within your faith community or beyond. These avenues can provide much-needed support during times of financial crisis and can be seen as the provision of God through the resources available to assist those in need.

The loss of a marriage partner is a profoundly challenging experience with both emotional and financial dimensions. However, from a biblical perspective, the wisdom of the Bible can provide invaluable guidance on how to cope with these financial trials. By assessing the financial impact, relying on God's provision, seeking support from your faith community, creating a new financial plan, and exploring financial assistance, you can navigate this difficult journey with faith, resilience, and the unwavering knowledge that God's grace will sustain you even in the face of profound loss.

Eternity

Why eternity? Well, because we are designed for eternity. Our life does not consist merely of our short life span here on earth but continues after our physical death.

In Ecclesiastes 3:11, Solomon said, "God has made everything beautiful in its time. Also, he's put eternity into man's heart yet so that he can really find out what God has done from the beginning to the end." But we have to do our best to try and find out what God has done, what God wants to do and how He will help us have an eternal impact with eternal results.

Imagine your life as a line, stretching from the moment you were conceived, not just physically in the womb but much earlier as a unique thought of God, to eternity. Your life on that line is a tiny dot. You are living in that dot right now, but if we're smart, we'll not live for the dot but for the line.

God is eternal; people will live forever, and His word will live forever. So, live your life now while you're in the dot, in light of the line, invest in the line. That's what's going to matter after you die.

Jesus said, "Do not store up for yourselves treasures on earth, where moths and vermin destroy, and where thieves break in and steal." (Matthew 6:19). Why is he telling them, don't store up for yourselves treasures on earth? Because they're not going to last.

Jesus says, turn it around. Store up for yourselves treasures in heaven.

If you know Jesus, you are going to heaven - then every day of your lives that you invest in treasures are in heaven, you are getting closer to those treasures instead of moving away from them. If you spend your life investing in treasures on earth, you've reason to despair. Jesus says moving towards your treasure, towards heaven, gives reason to rejoice.

Let's look at other reasons why Jesus tells us not to lay up treasures on earth.

Firstly, it is a poor investment. Moth and rust destroy them. The forces of nature are unstable, and decay and deterioration are built in. Inflation slowly takes away the value of our money. Identity theft and digital theft through phishing and many other types of deception can easily steal our assets. Governments' taxes and investments go sour.

Secondly, it affects the human spirit. Contentment and satisfaction are very fleeting. The joy at something new quickly disappears, leaving us wanting the next thing. We often fear the loss of what we rely on, be it a bank balance, possessions, or sufficient return on investments. There is usually an excessive need to preserve and protect.

Thomas Watson wrote, "The soul is a spiritual thing, riches are of an earthly extract, and how can these fill a spiritual substance? How man does thirst after the world, but, alas, it falls short of his expectations. It cannot fill the hiatus and longing of his soul."[11]

Randy Alcorn writes, "Materialism is the mother of anxiety. No wonder Christ's discourse on earthly and heavenly treasures immediately follows his warnings not to worry about material things. People lay up treasures on earth rather than in heaven not only because of greed and selfishness but also because of fear and insecurity. Yet putting our hope in earthly treasures does nothing but multiply anxiety. Why? Because earthly treasures are so temporary and uncertain." [12]

Martin Luther said, "There are only two days on my calendar. This day and that day." Every decision he made was based on these two days. He asked, how much is needed to get through today? But the most critical question is how can I use my money today, which will have maximum impact on that day when we will see Jesus again and start life with Him in eternity.

The Bible says before the judgment seat of Christ, there will be accountability. "For we must all appear before the judgment seat of Christ, so that each one may receive what is due for what he has done in the body, whether good or evil." (2 Corinthians 5:10). When we stand before the judgment seat of Christ, we will receive either a reward or something else we don't know about.

The sharper our vision is focussed on that day, the sharper our vision is on what will happen in eternity, and the better decisions we will make today in light of eternity.

My faith in Jesus determines my eternal destination, but my behaviour determines my eternal rewards.

C.S. Lewis wrote, "Indeed, if we consider the unblushing promises of reward and the staggering nature of the rewards promised in the Gospels, it would seem that Our Lord finds our desires not too strong, but too weak. We are half-hearted creatures, fooling about with drink and sex and ambition when infinite joy is offered us, like an ignorant child who wants to go on making mud pies in a slum because he cannot imagine what is meant by the offer of a holiday at the sea. We are far too easily pleased." [13]

He's asking us to focus more on these eternal rewards promised in the gospel, which Lewis describes as the 'staggering nature' of these rewards. So we need a sharp vision of eternity and the rewards laid before us, the promise of eternal rewards.

Will we be married in heaven?

The Bible conveys in Matthew 22:30, "At the resurrection, people will neither marry nor be given in marriage; they will be like the angels in heaven." This statement was made by Jesus when addressing a query about the marital status of a woman who had experienced multiple marriages in her earthly life (Matthew 22:23-28). It suggests that the institution of marriage, as we know it, won't exist in heaven. However, it's important to note that this doesn't imply that husbands and wives won't recognise each other in heaven. Furthermore, it doesn't negate the possibility of a deep and meaningful relationship between us in the heavenly realm.

However, anything we have done for each other here on earth will be taken with us as individuals into eternity. So, let us build each other up and help one another grow as Jesus' disciples. "And we all, who with unveiled faces contemplate the Lord's glory, are being transformed into his image with ever-increasing glory, which comes from the Lord, who is the Spirit." (2 Corinthians 3:18)

"But you, dear friends, by building yourselves up in your most holy faith and praying in the Holy Spirit, keep yourselves in God's love as you wait for the mercy of our Lord Jesus Christ to bring you to eternal life." (Jude 1:20,21)

The Author

Peter Briscoe is an Englishman, born in 1950, and studied Industrial Chemistry and Management at Loughborough University of Technology. He moved to The Netherlands in 1974 and was asked by his company to set up a subsidiary in Holland, selling chemical specialties to the aerospace and food processing industries.

From 1986 to 1990, Peter was Executive Director of CBMC, Christian Businessmen's Committees, in Holland.

In 1990, Peter set up "Synthesys". a consulting company specialising in chemical product development. When the Berlin Wall collapsed in 1990, Peter developed Europartners, a movement dedicated to reaching European business and professional leaders for Christ.

In 2002, Peter took an assignment as Managing Director of HE Space Operations, serving the European Space institutions, specialising in providing professional services for spaceflight activities.

In 2008, Peter retired from business to develop a movement of Biblical stewardship in Europe, first of all through Crown Financial Ministries and then Compass - finances God's way.

At home, Peter is a member of the Baptist Church of Leiden, and served twelve years as chair of the elder board.

He has been married to his Dutch wife, Didie, since 1972. They are blessed with three daughters, three sons-in-law, and six grandchildren.

About Compass

Compass - finances God's way is a global, non-denominational movement teaching financial discipleship and generosity. The purpose is to serve individuals, churches, businesses, ministries, schools and other organisations by providing biblically-based solutions for handling money and possessions. Our vision is to see everyone, everywhere, faithfully living by God's financial principles in all areas of their lives.

Compass's mission is to help people everywhere learn, apply, and teach God's financial and business principles. We are looking for three major outcomes.
- To know Christ more intimately.
- To become free to serve the Lord and our neighbours.
- To help to fulfil the Great Commission

The Compass Global Team is comprised of local leadership on six continents – Europe, Asia, South America, North America, Africa and the Indian subcontinent. Our continental offices serve more than 90 nations around the world. Compass is active in over 80 nations over the globe and has resources in many languages.

To see specific English language resources, please visit the US shop at **www.compass1.org** or the EU shop at **www.compass1.eu**

Bible Studies for the Family

A 6-part Bible Study for couples This study will improve your marriage and your finances. because you will be learning what God says about having a great marriage and handling money wisely together.

Money and Marriage God's Way is for everyone whether you're engaged, newly married or empty nesters

A Bible study with 9 chapters, each with a 6 day self-study part and extensive explanation notes. Navigating Your Finances God's Way is for everyone - single or married, young or old, whether you earn a lot or little. It covers these topics - God's part and my part; work, debt, honesty, counsel, lifestyle, investing, giving and eternity.

An activity book to teach children ages 7 and under, for use in the home, Children's Church and Christian Schools. Give, Save, Spend teaches God's way of handling money. Discover these truths as Alfie, Amy, Jack and Lebo try to save enough money to buy a puppy. As they find out how to earn, save, give and spend money they also learn some important things about God.

Teaching children from ages 8-12 about how to manage money God's way.

Follow the story of Nathan, Rosie, Luke and Bethany as they try to save enough money to go on a school trip to the mountains. Go with them as they learn to earn, give, save and spend money, and discover some important things about the Bible and God's ways with money and possessions.

Endnotes

1 C.S. Lewis in Mere Christianity, Chapter 6.

2 https://en.wikipedia.org/wiki/Patrick_Peyton

3 The Complete Marriage Book: Collected Wisdom from Leading Marriage Experts, by David & Jan Stoop. 2002. Fleming H. Revell. Co.

4 https://www.cnbc.com/2020/02/05/53-percent-of-americans-have-kept-money-secrets-from-their-partner.html

5 Dr. Emmerson Eggerich, "Love and Respect." 2005. Thomas Nelson.

6 Tomas Sedlacek, "Economics of Good and Evil: The Quest for Economic Meaning from Gilgamesh to Wall Street." Oxford University Press. 2013.

7 Anselm Grün. "Gier: Auswege aus dem Streben nach immer mehr." 2015, Vier Turme Verlag.

8 E.F. Schumacher. Small Is Beautiful: Economics as if People Mattered (Harper Perennial Modern Thought. (2010)

9 http://christianmotivations.weebly.com/christian-motivations-blog/in-the-midst-of-the-storm-by-beth-moore

10 https://www.desiringgod.org/messages/getting-old-for-the-glory-of-god

11 https://thepastorsworkshop.com/sermon-quotes-on-prosperity/

12 https://www.patheos.com/blogs/randyalcorn/2021/08/ten-ways-materialism-ruin/

13 C.S. Lewis, The Weight of Glory (First American Edition, Macmillan, 1949), pp. 1–3.

www.ingramcontent.com/pod-product-compliance
Lightning Source LLC
LaVergne TN
LVHW020051210726
843507LV00015B/1360